m

history of cannabis

marijuana for dopes

a pop culture history of cannabis

Joseph Romain

Warwick Publishing Inc.
Toronto Chicago
www.warwickgp.com

marijuana for dopes
a pop culture history of cannabis
©2001 Joseph Romain

We acknowledge the financial support of the Government of Canada through the Book Publishing Industry Development Program for our publishing activities.

ISBN: 1-894020-97-9

Published by **Warwick Publishing Inc.**
162 John Street
Toronto, Ontario M5V 2E5 Canada
www.warwickgp.com

Distributed in Canada by:
General Distribution Services Ltd.
325 Humber College Blvd.
Toronto, ON M9W 7C3

Distributed in the United States by:
LPC Group
1436 West Randolph Street
Chicago, Illinois 60607

Cover Design: Kimberley Young
Editor: Nick Pitt
Book Design: Clint Rogerson
Front Cover Cartoon: Harry "Fast Chicken" Young

Printed and bound in Canada

Table of Contents

Preface

THE NIGHT I DECIDED TO UNDERTAKE THE ASSIGNMENT TO WRITE THIS BOOK was the occasion of my friend Eric's fiftieth birthday.

Eric, the demi-centurian, is vice president of one blue-chip listed company and director of several others. He had invited a dozen or so neighbors in on a chilly winter night to help him celebrate, and we did so with dinner and wine and a rousing chorus of the birthday song. The Tex-Mex buffet was over and I was warming myself before a cheery fire in the front room. Eric's fine after-dinner brandy was doing for my insides what the fire was doing for my outsides. Life was good. I was musing quietly over whether I could afford to accept or reject the kind offer of my publisher to pay me to write this book.

I didn't think writing a book about marijuana was exactly in my line. I was, I calculated, an aspiring novelist, and I didn't really know that much about grass, except that most people I know have smoked some. Twenty-five years ago I marched against the Vietnam War, joined sit-ins on campus, and smoked joints before philosophy classes, but that's all ancient history. I remember one day at the University of Windsor I signed a petition to change the marijuana laws and the guy gave me a cool little button from the National Organization to Reform Marijuana Laws (NORML). I've still got the button, so I guess I have bona fide credentials to write this book about grass.

As I ruminated over these and other amusing considerations, Steve, a neighbor of Eric's who makes his living repairing the glass skins of high-rise buildings, tapped me on the shoulder and presented me with a more immediate dilemma. Steve the glazier passed me a marijuana cigarette. What should I do? Should I smoke it, or wave him off? I mean, this wasn't a Sarah McLachlan concert for heaven's sake, it was a neighborhood dinner party!

What the hell. I took a tentative puff and sheepishly proffered it in the direction of the man on my right, a secondary school mathematics teacher; he deftly disentangled it from my fingers, sucked it expertly, and passed it to Alan, an embarrassingly successful investment banker. Alan counted three quick toots from the joint and passed it to our host. He twiddled his mustache and grinned, wafting the smoke up into his nostrils — judging the bouquet of Steve's *ruderalis canadianis* — before taking a calculated toke.

At this very moment, Jemma, our hostess, doting mother of three lovingly spoiled children, came through the door, right on cue, and wagged her finger at the roomful of sheepish delinquents.

"Here you are, the pillars of bloody society, smoking stuff that could cost you all your jobs. They could put you behind bars, for heaven's sake!" Jemma relieved her husband of the burning twig, and I held my breath. Guilty as charged, your honor.

Jemma, whose university days were spent at Manchester, took a long drag on the reefer, shot us all a conspiratorial grin, and retreated to pass the vile thing among our wives.

I think it was Jemma who convinced me to write this book. She reminded me that the prohibition against marijuana is intentionally naive, unintelligent, and impossible.

It is intentionally naive since virtually all of the studies that have considered the physical, social, psychological, medical, and legal consequences of cannabis use have returned the same verdict: The prohibition of marijuana will cause more harm than marijuana itself ever could.

Prohibition is unintelligent, because it robs the human economy of much needed commercial, spiritual, and environmental benefits. It fills our court-

rooms with innocent citizens, and sends our children into the clutches of crime. The costs of enforcement are out of all sane proportion to the benefits of some elusive "drug-free society."

Finally, prohibition is impossible because people like to smoke pot. Accountants and teachers and dentists and nurses and high-rise glaziers use it at the end of the day or among friends to relax and be sociable.

Prohibition will always be impossible, because the vice president of a blue-chip corporation can smoke a joint at his fiftieth birthday party on a Tuesday night, and make intelligent decisions the following morning.

Jemma arrived, back-end first, through the swinging door to the front room. She found five men intensely involved in a discussion concerning local politics and school funding. The sounds of laughter from the back of the house and the smoldering ember between her fingers left no doubt about what the wives had been doing.

"Have you got any more of that horrid stuff?" she winked.

Of the five men in the room, three of them reached into their pockets and offered her their stash. Now, these are not jazz musicians or windshield wipers, these are "the pillars of bloody society": the butcher, the baker, and the candlestick maker. In Canada, where this scene unfolded, simple possession of grass is on the books as cause for a six-month retreat in the Mounties' cabin; if you grow the stuff, they can take away your house. And among the writers, librarians, engineers, teachers, high-wire guys, and financial analysts in the room, three of them produced pot.

So, capable librarian that I am, I went out and found out all about marijuana. I read books, magazine articles, and web sites, contacted a lot of people involved in the trade, and generally made a good job of the research. I confess up front that I smoked some.

What I found out about grass between that time and this will astound you. Grass is a big story. This isn't just something that happened in the 1960's. Cannabis and humans go back a very long way, and the story is fascinating. You will read of gods and poets who swore by it, nations ruled by it, and billions spent prohibiting it. It has been studied to death, tested ad nauseam, and is the preoccupation of millions of web crawlers who offer and seek information on the Internet.

This is a book for all the glaziers and dopers and singers and tax lawyers and mechanics and nurses and librarians and vice presidents and shipping clerks and teachers and accordion players, professors of Early American Literature, and grave diggers with whom I have shared a smoke. This is a book for the butcher, the baker, and the candlestick maker — even if they don't inhale.

Notes to the Reader:
Confessions and Disclaimers

The author confesses that he believes that prohibition is flatly immoral and impossible to enforce. Since prohibition plays such an important role in the life of Mary Jane, you will read a lot about it in this book. The author will attempt to bring you along into the anti-prohibitionist camp. He may resort to honest sophistry or even climb up on a soap box to do so. So be advised.

The author also understands that in some jurisdictions, selling, owning, or even reading this book may be a criminal offense, and so he suggests that if you are currently reading this in such a place, you must either stop reading, or go someplace else. Preferably the latter. In either case, he refuses to be held responsible for your criminal actions.

The author states, from the outset, that he does not suggest that any reader should ever smoke, eat, or otherwise ingest, cannabis drugs. Especially while reading this book. Some of this stuff gets pretty heady, and a reader will want his or her little gray cells functioning on all four cylinders. The decision to smoke cannabis is a personal one, and the author only wishes to provide his reader with information, scientific and otherwise, about the history and mental geography of the subject. He is an advocate only for freedom of personal choice, not for the use of mind-altering substances.

It is not the author's job to tell his reader what to smoke, or what to think. The author's job is to entertain, inform and provoke.

To make the individual uncomfortable, this is my task.

—*Nietzsche*

Chapter 1
What Is this Stuff, Anyway?

GRASS IS MORE THAN A NATURALLY OCCURRING EUPHORIC USED BY ANCIENT AND civilized people to relieve their frantic grip on reality. It is more than a byproduct of the ropemaking trade. And although it has been used by every sort of medicine man or woman in history, it is more than balm for the afflicted.

It is less than the bane or salve of all social ills, but it is a potent social catalyst. Grass is a symbol of defiance, a powerful creative stimulant, and was the emblem of the generation currently emerging into the halls of power. This humble weed defined a generation who fought the system and lost, brought whirling dervishes and trumpet players into states of rapture, and provided relief from hard reality in cultures where alcohol was taboo.

For the generation who fought for civil rights in the American south and peace in Vietnam, grass was a badge, and was generally present wherever two or more were gathered in protest or peace. On the other side of the ledger, governments have set new high-water marks in law-enforcement procurement budgets and low-water marks in trampling civil rights in their seemingly useless attempt to stop people from smoking grass. A conservative estimate of the cost, world wide, of enforcing prohibition of euphoric herbs is in the tens of billions of dollars annually — more than is spent on AIDS research, Interpol, and reforestation combined. The wisdom of this activity isn't the point here — though it is interesting that with all this money being spent people can still get their hands on the stuff — the point is that marijuana holds such a significant place in the hearts and minds of humankind that they will risk incarceration just to smoke a little reefer.

So What Is This Stuff that Binds Chums and Divides Generations?

The substance Americans and Europeans know as grass is, in a word, cannabis, though to say cannabis is not saying enough.

There are at least three distinct types of cannabis, and there is considerable disagreement over whether there are three (or more) distinct species, or whether there is one species with distinctive environmentally determined presentations. The three species, or presentations, are *Cannabis sativa, Cannabis indica,* and *Cannabis ruderalis.* The distinction among the three is not merely an esoteric argument among plant taxonomists (though it is certainly that as well), it has also formed the basis for lively legal defenses of those charged with possession of a prohibited substance: If it can be proven that a person charged with possession of *Cannabis sativa* was in fact in possession of *Cannabis ruderalis,* it might be, and has been, successfully argued that the defendant is not guilty of the charge. What we call pot seems to be important.

Linnaeus, who attempted to catalog the world of plants in the middle of the eighteenth century, classified grass as *Cannabis sativa,* after the Scythian name for the plant (cannabis) and the Spanish city known for its fine hemp paper products (Xativa). Later plant taxonomists have identified *indica* and *ruderalis* in other parts of the world (India and Africa, respectively), which has led to the argument over whether their later discoveries qualify as true species or merely variations of the plant described by Linnaeus. In the meantime, people went on smoking all three, without much thought being given to the subtleties of botanical classifications.

In fact, most people don't call it cannabis at all. They call it grass, or tea, or jive, or bud, or smoke, or pot, or boo, or kif, or smoke, or mezz, or weed. If the number of names for a thing is any indication of its cultural importance, then *cannabis whateveryoucallit* has got to rank among the top dozen or so substances known to humankind.

In America, and consequently in most of the world, grass is known as "marijuana." It was the term known to southern American law enforcement officials in the 1930's, and it was they who brought grass to the attention of the American people.

Though "hashish" was a word many Americans would have heard in various contexts, they didn't connect it with marijuana. "Marijuana" was some kind of Mexican loco weed. Nobody knew what "marijuana" was. In fact, when the Marijuana Tax Act was being pitched to congressmen and senators, nobody mentioned that "marijuana" meant "hemp," one of America's oldest and most profitable seed and fiber crops; and nobody went out of their way to tell the medical community that it also meant cannabis preparations, which were a common remedy in a doctor's kit bag. It was not until days before passage of the bill that the American Medical Association and the bird seed manufacturers' lobby learned that they were dealers in marijuana and that the legislation was going to seriously affect the way they did business.

Whatever Else Grass Might Be, It Is a Psychoactive Plant

It gets you high. It alters your perception of reality. Grass is hemp, of course, and it is among the oldest cultivated plants in history. If somebody tells you that hemp is marijuana's cousin, they are playing with the truth. Marijuana *is* hemp. It provided our forefathers and foremothers with clothing, food, accommodation, and comfort. It also, it has been argued, opened human eyes to the possibility of religion, magic, and contemplation.

Since well before recorded history, people have smoked, eaten, and drunk euphoric preparations of cannabis. The reasons for this are many, but seem to be rooted in the nearly universal human need to alter consciousness. In all cultures, at all times, some people felt the need to make use of recreational drugs. Cannabis is only one such solution, but it has eased the aching reality bone of many a weary human soul.

The euphoria can be light and carefree, but can also lead you into a dark world of paranoia and hallucination. Preparations of cannabis resins rank among the most powerful psychoactive drugs known to science or religion, and must be used with very great care, and never frivolously.

In its lightest forms, grass is used as a mild sedative, enjoyable in social situations, much in the way some people use wine or beer. The smoker may giggle, lose track of time, and feel relaxed and happy for a short while, then they will feel sleepy. This effect is gained from drinking *bhang* or from smoking a modest amount of grass.

In its stronger forms, the resins of cannabis constitute a very powerful somatic drug, capable of disintegration of the human identity, and very capable of sending the user into a state akin to ecstasy, or into a state hospital.

Euphoric Preparations

Euphoric preparations can be made from the leaves, flowers, and resin glands of the cannabis plant. The leaves are used to make edible intoxicants like bhang and cannabutter, the flowers are generally smoked in the form of ganja or marijuana, and the resin glands are made into hashish and hashish oil.

In some parts of the world, cannabis leaves are a plentiful and inexpensive source of mild intoxication. In India, drinking bhang is as common as a cuppa' tea in Somerset. In ancient Egypt, bhang was first enjoyed as a cool refreshment taken after a long day at the pyramids. Women the world over recommend this comforting drink to ease childbirth and menstrual difficulties.

Ghee, or clarified butter, is the perfect medium for the extraction of cannabinoids. Any cannabis cook worth his salt has a jar of cannabutter in the cupboard. Cannabutter is made by simmering chopped cannabis leaves, or "shake," in a pot of melted butter. The leaves and froth are skimmed from the caldron, leaving a golden green pot of, well, pot. This "gunja ghee" can be used for creating all manner of mildly intoxicating candies, cakes, and cookies.

And Ganja is Exactly…?

For thousands of years, in a surprising number of places, cannabis flowers have been known as *ganja*. In much of the world today, we call smokable cannabis "marijuana," but for most of human history, we have known it as ganja, or some variation of that name. The earliest references to ganja are found in the ancient Hindu texts of the Rig-Veda, which takes us back at least six thousand years.

Marijuana, or ganja, is a pungent mixture of tiny, dried-up leaves and even tinier resin glands. Usually it is greenish or brown and gold, though it can also be reddish, yellow, or nearly black. In general, the darker, spicier grass is more potent, though high-mountain pot with very little smell can be surprisingly strong. In many parts of North America and Europe, the cultivation of cloned sinsemilla plants has become a popular hobby and business practice. These super strains of resin-oozing buds have the highest concentration of tetrahydrocannabinol (THC — the most obvious chemical agent in cannabis flowers), but any true connoisseur of high-test cannabis would forego these newfangled, hydroponically produced marvels for a good, old-fashioned chunk of Kashmiri black hashish.

Hashish

Hashish has often been associated with the word *assassin,* but only by those who do not understand hashish. Those who do understand hashish know that a hashish eater is no more likely to conspire in political assassination than he is likely to become emperor (Presidents Clinton and G.W. Bush aside…). The hashish eater, or smoker, may come to believe he is the Prince or the Caliph, but he has neither the inclination nor the energy to stalk and kill princes and caliphs.

Hashish is produced by rubbing the live flower buds of cannabis and collecting their sticky resin, or by sifting the dried flowers through fine silk screens. Most of the active agents in cannabis reside in the resin glands, and when separated from the moderating influence of the ganja leaves, constitute one of the most potent of psychotropic sources ever identified.

Hashish is generally smoked in a small pipe, but it can also be rolled in cigarettes with tobacco or ganja, or it can be eaten. In Egypt and in northern India and Pakistan, sweet hashish confection, or Turkish Delight, is a delicacy served on very special occasions.

Hashish is generally dark brown or black, but it can be rusty red (from Lebanon, Turkey, or India), green (Morocco or Turkey), soft, gooey black (Nepal, Afghanistan, Kashmir, and Bhutan), or striped with white or brown opium (Afghanistan, Turkey, Kashmir). The color and texture are functions of the geography and the method of production. Soft, pliable hashish is hand pressed from the living buds of high-mountain cannabis flowers, while lighter, brittle hashish is produced by the sifting and pressing process used in the Middle East. The grail of the hashish connoisseur is Bhutanese or Nepalese temple balls. In myth, if not in truth, young Bhutanese women and children run naked through the cannabis fields and collect the sticky sap on their bodies. They scrape it off and collect it for later processing. The clumps of resin are rolled between the palms of the hands, sometimes for days or weeks, until a perfect, solid hashish ball about the size of a walnut is inspected and stamped by the temple priests as worthy. These temple balls, as they are known, are so pure that an experienced outsider would shudder at the idea of a second puff.

It is not an accident that holy men have known about hashish for a long time. Sufis swore oaths of silence regarding hashish and its secret gateway to the land of "Allah"; incense burners in ancient Canaan and Babylonia filled the temples of Baal and Ashira with the holy hashish smoke. Cannabis, as we will see, has played a significant role in the spiritual history of humanity, and hashish has always been regarded as the omega of psychoactive preparations.

T.H.C.

What is it that gives these various forms of cannabis preparations their kick? THC is often said to be the active ingredient in cannabis. This is not incorrect, but it is misleading. THC is one substance among a family of cannabinoids which conspire to befuddle and inspire the human consciousness. THC is found in high concentration in resin glands, while other active cannabinoids are in higher concentrations in the leaves and seeds. The concentrations of THC and other psychoactive agents is determined by the genetic properties of that particular plant and the conditions under which it is grown. While it is apparently agreed that THC governs the potency of the drug, biochemists and hippies assure us that the particularities of the high are largely determined by the other psychoactives. Drobinol, or synthetic THC, has none of the moderating influences of the other, naturally occurring cannabinoids and, as a result, sends users over the psychic edge without a parachute. This is why, when given the choice between pure THC and grass, most favor the cannabis flowers. Biochemistry has proven what every hippie always knew.

Chapter 2
Getting High Is Ancient History

THE RITUAL OF STANDING AROUND UNDER A STREETLIGHT SMOKING A REEFER is old. Ancient. The streetlight is new. It has replaced starlight and cooking fires, but the reefer part hasn't changed much for at least twelve thousand years. It is older than drinking wine or smoking tobacco, and as far as we can tell, it predates recorded history. The history of grass takes us into dreamtime; it takes us into myth and legend. We cannot examine each and every culture for whom smoking dope has been important — there are far too many of them — but we can have a quick look at some of the more interesting ones. The oldest confirmed use of cannabis was in China, so we will begin our brief tour of history on the banks of the Yang T'se River.

Ma in China

Everybody knows that paper was invented in China many years ago. Mythology tells us that paper was invented by a eunuch named Ts'ai Lun about two thousand years ago. It isn't a tough intellectual leap from the invention of paper to the supposition that the first paper maker, whoever he or she was, was familiar with its principal ingredient: ganja. So far as we know, there was no agricultural board measuring the THC content of the weeds growing along the banks of the Yang T'se River at the time, so the hemp that he used was probably potent. And it is not a long mental leap to assume that he was familiar with its euphoric effects.

When hashish is gathered and manufactured in rustic cultures, one method of making the stuff is to rub the live flowers and scrape off the gooey green or brown resin that sticks to one's hands. The sticky stuff is gathered up and further processed into some of the world's most potent hashish. Imagine our paper maker harvesting his stock from the fields, getting that sticky stuff all over his hands. Would he taste it? Probably. Would he like it? Indeed. History insists on it.

Even if he didn't deliberately lick the stuff off his fingers, he would have had gummy cannabinols all over his skin that probably would have seeped into his bloodstream and sent him messages from the gods whether he liked it or not. At the very least, our ancestral paper maker would have been aware that the unretted plant was good for more than writing his memoirs on.

The Chinese almost certainly knew about grass from very early on in human evolutionary history. They have been farming hemp for clothing and shelter since time began. It has been argued that hemp was the first agricultural crop; the crop that led hunter-gatherers to settle into seasonal communities in the first place. Its fruit and fibers provided the householder with shelter, fuel, clothing, and food. If our supposition that skin contact with the plant induces inescapable euphoria is plausible, then it follows that the bounteous crop also provided these early humanoids with a source of entertainment, and probably a source of religious contemplation as well. Some thinkers argue that it was cannabis which led to the development of self awareness in humans.

We know that the Chinese were familiar with the medicinal and spiritual properties of their favorite substance. They called it *Ma,* liberator of sin. They used grass to cure the sick, raise the dead, and cleanse houses. Human illnesses were believed to be caused by demons invading the body, and ancient shamans would waggle magic clusters of grass over the patient, or around the temple, in order to chase away the offending demon. Why would they use cannabis for this purpose? They could have used anything. But they used hemp. It seems very likely that they used cannabis because they knew and respected the euphoric magic of the plant. They believed Ma to be a source of power.

As with most sources of power, rich people want to control it. Such was the case with grass in ancient China. Grass is very "Yin": it induces solipsism. It induced people to sit and think, and sitting and thinking was not seen as useful to those who wanted people to work harder and ask fewer questions. Over the centuries, the use of grass as a euphoric has been recognized and enjoyed in many Chinese cultures, and though it is currently in disfavor, it is available, along with other forms of escape from drudgery, on the black market.

Bhang on in India

Nobody knows how long they have been using cannabis to get high in India. In some parts of the country, cannabis is very nearly a god. In fact, Siva, who is a god, recommends its use for recreational and devotional purposes. It was Siva who brought ganja to the people of the Hindus Valley to ease their burden and lighten their hearts. The ganja highway is a well-traveled on-ramp to the land of the gods.

Tens of millions of people regard the drinking of bhang as a sacrament. Bhang is a concoction of cannabis, opium, herbs, spices, and milk. The people of the Indian subcontinent all the way up into the Himalayas have used the euphoric properties of cannabis in religious and social circumstances since time out of mind.

At the turn of the 20th century, the occupying British forces had reason to believe that the local custom of drinking, smoking, and eating ganja and its derivatives might be an undesirable habit for the average Indian native. There was great poverty, overpopulation, and crime and some people suggested that perhaps the ganja was the cause of all the misery. In the civilized manner to which the Brits have been habituated, the British government commissioned an inquiry into the sociological, psychological, medical, legal, and economic consequences of controlling or prohibiting the use of hemp drugs. The British Indian Hemp Drugs Commission came forward with some interesting conclusions. Basically, they thought that smoking pot was a nasty habit, like smoking cigars or drinking coffee, but as it was well entrenched in local customs, and controlling it would be unpopular, expensive, and uncalled for. They chose the colonialist route instead — and taxed it.

Courage

Africa is the source of *Cannabis ruderalis,* arguably the most potent naturally occurring form of grass on earth. It has been observed that cannabis is not native to Africa, and was probably brought to the Dark Continent by Turkish mariners who jumped ship in the seventh century BCE. These early renegades from marine service assimilated with the local people and eventually came to be known to outsiders as the Hottentots. What makes the Hottentots so hot?

As it turns out, it wasn't, as the *Wizard of Oz's* cowardly lion tells us, courage; it was *dagga.* Grass. The Dutch slavers who settled the southern shores of Africa soon learned that the locals prized their dagga above all else save cattle. A cattle herd was the badge of office among the Hottentots, status being determined by the number of cows, bulls, and steers owned. But many cows or few, no Hottentot would be caught dead without a bag of dope dangling from his loin cloth. The Hottentots called it dagga.

In the mid 1600's the Dutch colonialists taught the Hottentots to smoke it. Previously, they had eaten their sacred plant, but when mixed with fine Dutch tobacco, it made a potent combination that the Hottentots took to like bees to honey. They made pipes from the horns of their prized cattle, and improvised water pipes of various sorts. On the other side of the ledger, the Dutch invaders delighted in the new source of intoxication and planted their own.

Cultivation of dagga in Southern Africa became an important part of governing the new Cape Colony. The loyalty of those natives who were pressed into farming or household service was ensured by the provision of dagga in sufficient quantities. It was used as a form of currency; the Dutch found it difficult to purchase cattle and labor, but with good dagga and Dutch tobacco, they could buy anything.

The Hottentots were not the only Africans smoking dope early on, however. Dagga cults existed in the north, in Ethiopia, where the mandatory practice of smoking grass was a religious sacrament as well as a form of governance. In some regions, crimes were punished by forcing the reprobate to smoke nauseating quantities of strong dagga until they admitted and showed contrition for their crimes. Or until they passed out. Members of the dagga community were required to greet each other with a sign of peace and brotherhood. They were not allowed to hold grudges or think ill of other community members. Every night, the men gathered and shaved their heads before entering the circle, where they smoked dagga and confessed their sins. Many years later, astonished anthropologists found that the dagga cults had brought peace to warring tribes, dissipated the harsh tribute system of the rule of the fiercest, and gave rise to trade among former mortal enemies.

Some adherents to the Ethiopian Zion Coptic Church, of which we will hear more in a later chapter, believe that the real sacrament Jesus brought to humankind was the baptism by smoke. They call the holy herb Lamb's Breath, and revere its euphoric qualities for its gift of transcendence.

Africa is a vast, warm place with rich soils, unspoiled wilderness and diverse cultures. In many of these lands, grass has been prohibited, and in some places, the prohibition has been effective. However, where there is lush and fertile ground, and people who want to smoke grass, there will be grass.

Persian Paradise

Cannabis intoxication has been practiced by the people of the Middle East and North Africa since at least 1200 BCE. The Prophet directed the Muslim peoples to eschew alcohol, but apparently since He said nothing about grass, many Islamic holy men and lay people have taken the scripture's silence as tacit permission. Throughout the Muslim world, various forms of cannabis preparations are used for sacred and mundane euphoria by millions of people.

The story of the monk Hayder is probably not true in literal terms, but it is old enough to be called legend, and is peculiar enough to be worth retelling.

Hayder, a Dervish, or monastic Muslim, spent many dour years eating gruel and kneeling on rocks in central Persia, where we can presume he explored the great and small questions of life and paid homage to God. He is said to have been a melancholy monk who kept to his own small room and took no obvious joy in his devotion. We can imagine that any joy would have been difficult to identify, but his fellow hermits, who gave us the story, found it important to tell us that he was a gloomy Sufi.

One day, Hayder returned from his morning constitutional in an uncharacteristically gleeful state. He greeted his fellows with a smile and invited them into his room for a bowl of tea. The fellows were dumbfounded, but they followed. He served them tea, and swore them to silence. We can imagine Hayder breaking out the secret stash of tea from behind a rock and brewing up a potful for his fellow travelers on the ascetic road. "I have found a secret," he might have told them, "and a secret it must remain. I will tell you all on condition that you do not reveal the secret to those outside the devotion of Allah, the Sufis."

He told of how he was walking, meditating, when his attention was drawn to the tall, graceful weed that seemed to dance and sway in the sunlight. He broke off a flower and wafted its pungent bouquet into his face. He tasted it, and found it lugubrious on his palate, but spicy and not unpleasant. He tasted some more, chewing the soft, peppery flower bud. It was not long before he began to feel elated, and he returned to the happy plant. He found that as he rubbed his hands over the leaves and flowers, a dark green resin gathered on his palms, and he could scrape this gum into a ball. Hayder had discovered hashish.

The Whirling Dervishes have never looked back. The music, the whirling, and for some, the hashish, is the portal to the lands of God.

Egypt

Egypt has always been a hub of human activity. Since the business of civilization has been recorded, Egypt has played an important role in culture, religion, technology, and esoteric knowledge. As one would expect, it has played a central role in the export of cannabis culture, and it was from Egypt that the West derived its knowledge of ganja — or kif as Egyptians call it.

Preparations of cannabis were certainly known to medical men and midwives in Egypt since time began, and it is difficult to imagine that the Egyptians, who traded with everyone — Africans, Mediterraneans, Persians — would have been unaware of the euphoric properties and religious ceremonies associated with it.

The low-brow habit of hashish consumption has been viewed as a problem in Egypt since the days before the pyramids. The poor people like to smoke it, and the rich people don't want them to, so they introduce prohibitions.

The Sultan of Turkey, who ruled Egypt in the mid 1800's, was not at all happy about the number of Egyptians who where smoking and eating vast quantities of hash and passing their days in a coma-like state. Comatose workers don't get much done. And there must have been a lot to do, since the Sultan made possession of hashish a capital offense in 1868.

A remarkably enthusiastic series of prohibitive measures were unleashed, culminating in the death sentence. The interesting thing is that although the prohibition verged on maniacal, it had little effect on the consumption patterns along the banks of the Nile. In Egypt, the people who smoked dope were either wealthy, and therefore above the law, or poor, and had little to lose but their miserable lives. When possession of a finger-sized chunk of hashish or a pouch of kif became punishable by immediate execution, there was no discernible decrease in the number of people buying and selling it. Among the avid customers were the French mariners who had arrived with Napoleon. These seafarers carried their hashish habit back with them to the ports of France, whence it was imported to the cultural capital of Paris.

Chapter 3
Pot in Europe and the West

IN 1807, NAPOLEON SIGNED A TREATY WITH THE RUSSIAN CZAR ALEXANDER which, in exchange for alliance with France, ended all trade between Britain and Russia. This Treaty of Tilsit was important enough to put the British fleet into action in defense of their trade rights with Russia. The Royal Navy, under Lord Horatio Nelson, set out in jig time, sails billowing and guns at the ready. Patriotic young lads in search of adventure and glory lined up to serve under the great admirals of the day: Lord Nelson on one side of the Channel and Napoleon Bonaparte on the other. Some of them found death at sea, and some of them found other sorts of glory, as we will see. The Treaty of Tilsit was a significant international trade agreement, and resulted in the horrible death of many British and French soldiers and seamen, but why are we concerned about it here in a book about grass?

For a couple of reasons, most obviously because the chief product under international contraband was cannabis. Without cannabis, the British were sunk. It's not as though Britain was a nation of pot heads, however. Napoleon and Nelson staged their conflict on water, and in order to float all that hardware, they needed rope. A lot of rope. You get rope from cannabis.

And the Russian steppes were home to the world's largest and sturdiest cannabis plants. If Britain didn't have access to the Russian hemp fields, their proud and mighty navy would fall apart at the seams, quite literally, leaving the French to command the seas.

Just like everybody else, Lord Nelson found ways around the prohibition of trade in cannabis. He organized the production of hemp in Canada, the West Indies, and in friendly South American countries, thereby entrenching the evil weed among agricultural workers throughout the British Empire.

For their finest ropes and sails, however, the Brits had need of the finely crafted product from the Steppes. Nelson devised all manner of ways to get the fine hemp out of Russia. The British engaged American merchant ships — sometimes at gun point — to haul the hemp across the French lines. It was costly, but the Royal Navy depended on it. The Czar and his customs officers turned a blind eye; illegal trade was profitable, even if it cost Czar Alexander France's friendship.

Napoleon decided to take control of the hemp fields himself, and invaded Russia in the ill-fated campaign of 1812. By the winter, most of the hemp had been woven and exported, and the French invaders were frozen, sick, starved, or dead before the spring. Napoleon retired from Russia with his tail between his legs, and the rest, as they say, is history.

The comings and goings of Napoleon and his navy are important to us for another reason. Roaming about the Mediterranean brought sailors and officers into contact with sights and sounds far beyond their imaginings. French and British fighting ships would regularly make calls in the wondrous ports of Cairo, Tripoli, and Istanbul, where former farm boys and dock workers encountered Arabs and Moors, Dervishes and Africans, fine silk and exotic foods. Men returned from the campaigns of Nelson and Napoleon with tales of wonder, fragrant spices, and hashish.

Pass the Majoon

Among the more extraordinary treasures brought home by seafaring entrepreneurs was *majoon* of various sorts. Majoon is a concoction of strong cannabis resins prepared as jams or confections, and there was a quiet but significant trade in these products in clandestine quarters all over Europe. In the mid 1800's, it was popular among European gentry at college or club, as well as having its regular customers at dockside grog houses and pharmacies. In the early 1850's, hashish found its way from Greece, or Egypt, or Lebanon, and into the hands of Dr. Jacques Joseph Moreau de Tours.

It is tempting to argue that Dr. Moreau and his Club des Hachichins, which included some of Paris's waxing literary lights, unveiled the secret of the Sufis to the masses, but it would be saying more than is true. However these influential pioneers of the nether-regions of euphoria are to be awarded due commendation for drawing the attention of the wealthy and influential to a pleasure that had hitherto been a well-known secret among the poor.

The Club des Hachichins

The first recorded European pot parties were held by the Club des Hachichins, who met monthly at an elegant Latin Quarter estate, the Hotel Lauzun. Among its members was Gustave Flaubert, one of France's leading men of letters and author of *Madam Bovary.* Flaubert was a driven artist who strove for perfection in his craft. His minute observation of human affairs and his ability to understand and convey the motives of the human spirit are what set him apart from his many gifted contemporaries. Given his rococo taste for detail, it is not difficult to understand his fascination with hashish intoxication. Also among the group was rebel poet Charles Baudelaire, whose *Flowers of Evil* would make any modern-day Jim Morrison seem tame indeed.

At a meeting of the Club des Hachichins, the group would eat some hash, have dinner, and settle into sumptuous leather armchairs to hallucinate for several hours while the good doctor Moreau took notes. The doses served up by Moreau de Tours were concocted from prime Lebanese or Turkish hashish, pistachio nuts, dates, lemon peel and other sumptuous ingredients, blended into a delectable pâté. It was described as a greenish lump of paste, about the size of a man's thumb, and Flaubert was told that it was "to be deducted from your share of paradise." Indeed. Imagine eating a clump of fine hashish that weighs between 10 and 15 grams. It's no wonder the club met only once a month.

Imagine having dinner with Honoré de Balzac, Théophile Gautier, Charles Baudelaire, and Gustave Flaubert — virtually every important author from the early modern period of Parisian literature — and observing their descent into hashish-induced madness. These fellows weren't gathering for a social smoke and witty conversation; they were taking more hashish than a normal person might smoke in a year or a lifetime. The fire crackled in the hearth while the poets cackled in the corners.

Moreau de Tours and the Club des Hachichins were truly a collaboration between art and science. The writers explored the effects of hashish intoxication through their writing, and Moreau de Tours produced a significant study of the psychiatric applications of cannabis drugs. The good doctor was interested in the causes and cures for madness; it was his belief that the ingestion of large quantities of hashish temporarily produced the symptoms of madness. His work with the Club des Hachichins resulted in the publication of *Hashish and Mental Illness*. For Baudelaire, what the drug produced was a *paradise artificiel*; his volume of the same name concludes that the wonders of hashish are a fool's paradise, but the sale of the book didn't hurt his reputation a bit.

While the works of Baudelaire, Flaubert, and Balzac remain on the syllabi of most modern institutions of higher learning, the works of Jacques Joseph Moreau de Tours have been scuttled away into the abyss of forgotten science. It was a hundred years before the likes of Timothy Leary and Tom Wolfe took an interest in madness and psychedelics and resurrected the work of Moreau de Tours.

Roll Britannia

It was not only in France that the ancient euphoric was gaining interest among artists and intelligencia. Lord Nelson's legacy was brought into intellectual and artistic circles in London, where the great artists of the day were dabbling in majoon, hashish, opium, and Caribbean cigars. The English Romantic Poets (a term of different meaning then and now) — amongst the greatest poets in any language — included some famously veteran drug abusers such as Coleridge, Blake, Byron, and even innocent and sweet John Keats himself.

Member of Parliament David Urquhart published his accounts of experiments with hashish in a tome he called *The Pillars of Hercules: A Narrative of Travels in Spain and Morocco* in 1848. What was good enough for an MP seemed to be fair game for the subjects of the realm. Adventurous academics and student seekers at Cambridge University, and presumably other European institutions of higher learning, were spending their allowance and their spare time munching squares of Turkish Delight, Bird's Tongue, Sesame Sweetmeat, and Crocodile's Penis, all strong concoctions of hashish, spices, gelatin and sugar. These confections were being cooked up in Egypt, Turkey, and Afghanistan, and shipped across Europe to impetuous upper class adventurers.

Although first-hand knowledge of hashish and its cousins was extremely limited, that didn't inhibit interest among the literati. Hashish and opium became popular devices for scribes to use as garnish or grist for their penny dreadfuls and medical journals. Drug-induced hallucinations became de rigeur in the literature of the day, and its study maintained a persistent undercurrent of medical investigation. Hashish was conceived as an aphrodisiac, a mystical gateway to heaven or hell, a poet's portal to publication, and as the most adaptable remedy for illnesses since cocaine.

Hashish in America

The oriental delights were haute cuisine on the Continent and in Britain, but they were not unknown in America. New York was then, as it is today, a destination of choice for people from every part of the globe. Some of them brought their customs of euphoric indulgence with them, and by the late

1800's, majoon, hashish, and ganja were available through importers of exotica and at hashish houses around the country. Hashish houses were probably far more numerous than can be documented, but they are known to have existed in New York, Chicago and Detroit. Their customers sought sumptuous environs, exotic hospitality, and strong, narcotic-quality hashish. A visit to the hashish house was a luxuriant and expensive indulgence, confined to the well-to-do or extravagant seeker.

Dr. H. H. Kane, M.D., brought hashish to the masses in *Harper's Magazine* in November of 1888 and whetted the appetite of America's avant-garde. *A Hashish House in New York: The Curious Adventures of an Individual Who Indulged in a Few Pipefuls of the Narcotic Hemp* is a lurid and enticing account of his visit to a bohemian hashish den on the dark side of New York City. This succulent little exposé did for hashish of the 1880's what *The Electric Kool-Aid Acid Test* did for psychedelics in the 1960's. America turned on.

Hashish and its cousins were freely transported between most countries, and those people who arrived in America brought their custom of smoking it with them. The use of euphoric herbs among "Syrians and Hindoos" was generally known and ignored by Americans until the 1930's, when the American preoccupation with prohibition was born.

Use of grass among African Americans became an issue in the late 1920's and early '30's, but they had been using it a long time by then. Most Africans did not exactly go to America willingly, and we can imagine that some of them were gladdened to find the pungent respite known by their fathers and the birthing herb of their mothers growing wild on the river banks of Babylon. They knew it by many names, and knew more uses for it than the slavers who owned them ever heard of. They remembered dagga.

How long the aboriginal peoples of North and South America have been using grass as a euphoric is a point of some disagreement among anthropologists and among First Peoples themselves. While some botanical historians argue that *Cannabis sativa* is native to the Americas, others insist that it was brought by any number of explorers, slaves, settlers, or migrating birds. Some Native Americans will tell you that cannabis was mixed with tobacco and other herbs during religious ceremonies; others will tell you that they never heard of the stuff. Any or all of these things might be true, and the various camps may never agree, but what is known is that Native Americans have used psychoactive plants since forever, and if cannabis was available, they were probably using it.

Chapter 4
Cannabis in the New World: Marijuana

CANNABIS HAS ENJOYED A PECULIAR CAREER IN NORTH AMERICA. AS NOTED in the previous chapter, nobody really knows how long people have been smoking it on this side of the world; the jury is still out in the court of American anthropology. But as a social issue, the "marijuana problem" can be clearly traced back to its prohibition under the Marijuana Tax Act of 1937. Prior to the Act, there was cannabis, and people smoking it, but there was no problem. Once it earned the honor of government disfavor, cannabis came into bloom. The prohibition of cannabis created an underground industry and an army of drug warriors to fight it.

Curious Lexicography

Though there are hundreds of words for cannabis in North America, the preferred term is "marijuana." If you look in an American dictionary, all of the other terms, including "cannabis," refer you back to "marijuana." It is fairly unusual in the lexicographical world for one slang term to become the point of reference for older and more reputable handles, and this should lead us to ask questions. How did this come to pass? Where did we get this word, and why has it surpassed all other slang terms in the race for etymological respectability?

The story of the word "marijuana" is more than idle etymology, however. It is the saga of how a lowly herb, employed by cowpokes and Mexican midwives, became Public Enemy Number One in the land of the free and the home of the brave. Cannabis flowers have for many years' running been America's top-ranking cash crop, and their production, distribution and the consequent law enforcement activities provide employment for more people than any other industry, legal or illegal. None of this might have been possible without the word "marijuana."

Why Do You Think They Call It a Roach?

In Mexico, like nearly everywhere else, a lot of people smoke *canamo*. Hombres roll it up in fat cigarettes and pass them around after a hard day of work. Women have traditionally used canamo as a balm for their bodies and a respite from grinding reality. Canamo is Spanish for cannabis, but like most other people who smoke cannabis, Mexicans don't call it by its proper name, they use code: *El diablito, fraho, Rosa Mari, Santa Marta* and *Mari Juana.*

In the mid 1910's Pancho Villa led a rag-tag band of Mexican freedom fighters against the encroachment of the United States into Mexican territory. His doings are remembered with affection and sentimentality in Mexico, but in the US he has become a figure of ridicule: the ultimate "munchie buster" has become a cartoon taco huckster, the Frito Bandito. Soldiers in Pancho Villa's army smoked canamo. But they didn't call it canamo, they called it Mari-Juana, or Mary-Jane, and it is from these guerrillas that we get the word "marijuana." The Tex-Mex folksong *La Cucaracha,* known to virtually every American with a pulse, was one of Villa's men's favorite marching songs. It is a song about marijuana. In fact, it is a song about not having any more marijuana. *La Cucaracha* is an ode to a burning ember. Why do you think they call it a "roach"?

La cucaracha, la cucaracha
Ya no puede caminar
Porque no tiene, porque le falta
Marihuana que fumar.

> (The little cockroach, the little cockroach
> He can't march anymore
> Because he wants, and hasn't got,
> [any] Marihuana left to smoke)

Muggles Magic

The Mexicans weren't the only North Americans smoking dope in the days of yore, however; it has long been known among the sons and daughters of Africa.

In the early 20th century, life among the displaced free Blacks in southern cities was unimaginably difficult. For those freed slaves who did not choose to go north, freedom from bondage meant grinding urban poverty in New Orleans, El Paso, and other southern cities. Those who were lucky enough to find employment at all worked at low-life cleaning jobs and backbreaking dockside labor. Crime was rampant. When you put hordes of people cheek by jowl in a shanty town, and demand that they make "bricks without straw," violence and passions will inevitably erupt.

So will music, and it erupted with a vengeance in New Orleans. The roots of jazz go back to the clash of African and European culture, of course, but jazz was largely born in the smoky Storyville section of New Orleans where brothels and bordellos predominated. Early jazz men smoked "moota" or "muggles" and tried to make sense of the freedom they had won. History tells us that misery is the mother of music, and jazz serves as a case in point. The pains and joys of a people were transformed into an idiom: jazz.

History also tells us that our grass grows along the ditches of poverty and desperation. Life is hard, and weed makes it less so. It makes people feel good. In the American south, it has always been available, inexpensive, and popular. Jazz players smoked it, and so did anybody else who had a nickel and need for an hour's time-out from reality. Smoking moota or "gage" was common in Storyville juke joints. White folk didn't even know about it, for the most part.

Eventually, though, white people caught on. Oscar Nowling, president of the Louisiana State Board of Health put two and two together and got five. He was concerned about the desperate condition of life among the urban poor. It was violent, disruptive, and they were playing all this weird music. In 1915, he told the governor and the surgeon general that marijuana was the source of violence and disorder. "Over two hundred children under fourteen are believed to be addicted to the marijuana habit."

Newspapers love this stuff. Lurid stories of drugs and violence sell newspapers. "El Paso Texas Bans Marijuana" got people reading. The city ordinance was brought into effect following a brawl between a group of white teenagers and a group of Mexican teenagers who had been smoking pot. Considering the social relations between Latino and white teenagers in El Paso in 1915, marijuana wouldn't rank high on my list of possible causes for the violence.

More limp stories ran under yellow headlines like "California Prohibits Marijuana Use Fearing Another Chinese Opium Scare," and "Louisiana Bans 'Mexican Killer Weed'." Marijuana became a focus for a thinly veiled racist attack on those people who employed it: poor Blacks and Hispanics. The first shots were fired in the War on Drugs.

Habitual Prohibition

In the late 1910's, America was entering the age of prohibition. American legislators were enthusiastically moving to outlaw all the vices of the nation. Prohibitionists were lobbying to ban cigarettes, opium, booze, and even jazz itself. While not all of these moves were successful, some of them were.

The Volstead Act, signed into law in spite of Woodrow Wilson's attempt to veto the bill, made the sale of alcoholic beverages a federal offense in 1919. In the ensuing dozen years, a small army of special agents and prosecutors were hired to enforce an almost universally unpopular prohibition of alcohol, while another army of producers, distributors, and middle men made fortunes selling fire water for big dollars. Some of America's biggest industries were created in the war against moonshine and malt, not the least of which was the Federal Bureau of Narcotics.

In 1933, America gave up the idea of prohibiting alcohol. New legislation allowed the sale of beer and wine as long as a tax was paid to the federal and local governments. The hey-day of Al Capone and Elliot Ness was passing into legend, and there was increasingly less work for booze busters. The crooks were crossing over into respectability and there was little to do but chase the rum and whiskey runners. What's a cop to do when his crooks become solid citizens? One thing they did was sign up with the Federal Bureau of Narcotics: the narcs.

Gunslinger Anslinger

Harry Anslinger was an ambitious copper in the rum-raiding business. He made good busts, and talked about them to anybody who would listen to and print his lurid stories. As deputy commissioner, his career was coming in to full bloom just as the laws were changing and the bootleggers were moving into main street. But Harry Jacob Anslinger had an uncle in government. Uncle Andrew was Andrew Mellon, king of the US treasury department and Standard Oil — so Harry got a pretty good job with the FBN: they made him the boss.

Anslinger's first job was to track down and prosecute heroin users. Following junkies and quack doctors was not very exciting or colorful work for a guy whose last job was racing through warehouses with a tommy gun. The fact is that there was not really a big problem with heroin abuse in America. Business was pretty slow.

It wasn't like the old days of chasing wing-tipped gangsters across state lines. It was hard to justify anything like an army to fight a handful of dazed junkies and prostitutes. But Harry had a knack for bureaucracy, and a drive for power. He was a consummate communicator, and he was well-connect-ed enough to have his stories run in William Randolph Hearst's string of daily papers. His racy accounts of the tragedy and mayhem in drug dens from New York to San Francisco won him the public profile and budget allo-cations he was after. But it still wasn't enough. Anslinger and his fledgling army needed a bigger enemy, so they invented one: *marijuana*.

Now, Anslinger didn't really think grass was a big deal. He told the Senate this on several occasions. He didn't think marijuana contributed, in any sig-nificant way, to the narcotics problems in America. But when he suddenly changed his tune, he did it in spades, publishing a string of made-up stories and half-truths about murder in Miami and Arabian assassins. After having told the Senate that marijuana wasn't on his list of priorities, he suddenly lunged out on an international campaign to outlaw all forms of cannabis, all over the world.

It is difficult to know what changed Harry Anslinger's mind about mar-ijuana. The history books tell us that Anslinger was just a very hard-nosed, if misguided, copper who truly believed that marijuana was evil. A cynic might point to the immediate augmentation of his narcotics control budg-et, now that a new enemy had been identified. There were thousands of Mexicans and Blacks and jazz musicians to round up, and this important work cost money!

The Grassy Knoll

Some people with suspicious minds connect Anslinger's sudden passion for stamping out cannabis with the emergent economic potential of hemp. The technology for making hemp viable as a fuel to rival petrochemicals and as a replacement cellulose in the manufacture of clothing and paper was the sub-ject of much scientific and industrial research. These suspicious people might make much of the proximity in time of the first hemp decordicator (a machine to spin hemp into gold: fabric and paper), the patent registration for nylon, and the prohibition of cannabis.

This leads to the question of how well connected Anslinger was to the treasury department through his uncle Andrew, to the petrochemical and other "backbone industries," also through his uncle Andrew, and to the Hearst newspaper empire. These people all had very powerful motives for the eradication of the industrial applications of the cannabis plant, and they had nothing to do with whether anybody smoked it or not. This stuff could provide viable competition to the textile, petrochemical, paper, and pharmaceutical industries.

Whatever his rationale, once he began his war on marijuana Anslinger was a tireless campaigner. His newspaper stories, thundering speeches, and healthy budget allocations made him undisputed czar of the drug enforcement world until Kennedy retired him in the early 60's. Before Anslinger was finished, he had managed to build his rag-tag battalion of bootleg busters into the vast army of prohibition enforcement that exists today. In his wake, however, is a vast criminal empire that is underpinned by the laws he created, and a hobbled industrial infrastructure. As the army grew, so did the consumption — hardly Anslinger's intention — but telling of basic human behavior.

Anslinger's act, the Marijuana Tax Act of 1937, was a watershed moment in bureaucratic history. Viewed 60 years later, it appears to have been a brilliant move to evade American federal legal tradition and to bring an emerging industry to its knees.

The federal government didn't really have the right to prohibit something like cannabis plants, but they did have the right to tax it. So the Marijuana Tax Act of 1937 called for the taxation of cannabis plants to the tune of a hundred dollars an ounce.

Now, these days, a hundred dollars for an ounce of good cannabis is a pretty fair price; people would probably be willing to pay that much tax for it, but when America was scrabbling out of the Great Depression, you would be hard pressed to find many a viper with a hundred dollars to spend on a bag of grass. So the tax was a virtual prohibition of pot. But it was also a virtual prohibition of any industrial applications of cannabis plants as well.

How could you make paper, or cotton, or paint, or food out of cannabis plants if the tax was a hundred dollars an ounce? Well, you couldn't. The Act actually included provisions to allow the production of hemp products, but they were cumbersome and confusing enough to make hemp farming look pretty unattractive. More important, doctors could no longer prescribe it to patients with nervous disorders, or pain, or depression: At a hundred dollars an ounce, sick people couldn't afford cannabis plants either.

The Pot Heads of the time really didn't have much of a voice in government, so their displeasure with the new law only had the effect of sending them underground to score their gauge. Nobody ever paid anything like a hundred dollars for an ounce of moota, but the money that did change hands was considerable, untaxed, and nurtured a small-time criminal underworld.

What is surprising is the silence of the hemp growers and doctors and textile trades on the issue. This seems strange, when you consider that cannabis extract was a standard part of a doctor's kit at the time, and that *Popular Mechanics* had touted hemp as the next big industry in America. Hemp farming had, after all, been a significant American enterprise since the pilgrim days. The deafening silence over the virtual prohibition of cannabis plants was remarkable. America was unaware of the restriction of hemp production until after the law prohibiting it had been signed into law.

The Bait and Switch

This brings us back to etymology. How would farmers, doctors, weavers and millers know that "marijuana" meant hemp? Remember that in 1937, nobody connected "marijuana" with cannabis plants or hemp oils. Well, almost nobody. The bird seed manufacturers' lobby knew about it, and, at the last moment, the American Medical Association figured it out.

When the bird seed boys found out that their product was going to cost more than the value of the stock they were feeding, they hit the roof! Their lobbying efforts resulted in a provision allowing them to import as much seed as they needed, at the old prices, as long as the seeds were sterile.

The American Medical Association didn't fare so well as the bird feeders, though. After having won a protracted and bitter fight over state Medicare, the AMA man, Dr. William Woodward, learned that the Marijuana Tax Act would mean that physicians could no longer prescribe cannabis, one of the standard remedies of the time. The AMA considered this an unwarranted intrusion into their professional realm. Woodward was allowed to make a deposition to the congressional committee studying the Act. He presented arguments that would have required months or years of study. It wasn't as though Woodward or the AMA were "soft on drugs"; their real concern was the intrusion of the government into the professional practice of medicine. The committee told him that if he couldn't help them get on with the business of passing this darned act, he should pack up and get out!

Why would congressmen vote for a law that eliminated one of America's longest-standing agricultural products? George Washington was a hemp farmer, for heaven's sake! Is it possible that the government of the day believed that George Washington was involved in the production of narcotics? Of course not. They just didn't know that "marijuana" was hemp. Nobody told them. In the House of Representatives, where the final vote took place, only one question was asked about the Marijuana Tax Act, and the answer speaks volumes:

> *Mr. Snell:*   What is the bill?
>
> *Mr. Rayburn:*   It has something to do with something that is called
>   marihuana. I believe it is some kind of narcotic.

If there was a conspiracy of industrialists and empire-building drug czars to make hemp and cannabis unavailable to the public, as is believed by many students of the subject, then it was brilliant. By using the northwest Mexican idiom "marijuana," Anslinger and company obscured the real nature of the bill they were passing. Whether this ban on hemp and its associated benefits was orchestrated by Andrew Mellon and William Randolph Hearst or not, it has had the effect of eliminating the industrial applications of the cannabis plant, while creating an ever-growing need for law enforcement personnel. And they could never have done it without Pancho Villa and his Cucaracha.

Anslinger Goes Multinational

Though the Marijuana Tax Act of 1937 may have provided Anslinger and America with an enemy the size of his ego and talents, it was still not enough. Anslinger and company felt the need to engulf the entire civilized world in their peculiar campaign against cannabis plants. Their efforts would culminate in international treaties whereby all signatories are responsible for the eradication of cannabis plants in their jurisdictions.

Here Comes the Man with the Jive

Meanwhile, despite the new legislation, the production and use of grass for recreational purposes continued unabated. When jazz moved north to Chicago, grass moved north with it. Chicago made a home for both. Players like Louis Armstrong and Tampa Red brought a new sound to the Windy City, and they brought grass along to help introduce the new southern feel. Now, there had probably been tokers in Chicago prior to the arrival of jazz, but most historians trace the migration of the marijuana habit up from New Orleans and Texas to Chicago, and from there to New York. Grass went wherever jazz went. In his classic autobiography, Mezz Mezzrow tells us that's exactly how it happened, and he should know, since he was the man with the jive.

Mezz Mezzrow was born in Chicago, the son of a nice Jewish mother and father. Mezz got himself on the wrong side of the law and grew up quick in holding cells and reform schools. By the time he graduated to real prisons, he had made himself out to be an "honorary negro," insisting he be locked up in the black cell blocks. He learned to play jazz clarinet passably well and he learned all about grass. You can hear Mezz on re-releases in better jazz record stores, but his real legacy to the genre was as the supplier of fine jive to the hippest cats in Harlem.

Mezzrow moved up the street to New York City, continuing to live where he was comfortable: outside the mainstream of straight, white society. He got gigs with mixed bands and with all-black bands, and was known and loved by jazz players of every hue. But whatever jazz players thought about Mezzrow's skin tone, or his clarinet playing, he was loved for his role as the best moota man in town.

Mezz Mezzrow is memorialized in jazz classics by such luminaries as Cab Calloway, Duke Ellington, Louis Armstrong, Bessie Smith, and the Mississippi Sheiks. Mezzrow would perch outside the coolest hangouts for jazz players and listeners and sell reefers at "two fo' a haf." Mezzrow made it his vocation to supply jazzmen with the finest gauge he could lay hands on, and with his prison connections, he could always get the best. In Harlem, among jive talkers, if something was "mezz" it was reliable, the best available, the real McCoy.

> *Dream about a reefer five feet long*
> *Mighty Mezz, but not too strong,*
> *You'll get high, but not for long,*
> *If you'se a viper.*
>
> — Fats Waller

Hemp on the Ropes

So Anslinger's marijuana ban had little effect on its ostensible target — a supposedly dangerous mind-altering substance — but effectively shut down other important industries. Just how important became apparent a few years after the Marijuana Act's passage, with the entry of the United States into the Second World War. If you are going to fight a war, you need rope. And the best rope comes from the same place as the best dope. Now, you can make rope from any number of plant fibers, but everybody knows that the best rope is made from cannabis plants. Even the United States government knows this. In 1942, America needed rope for the war. In fact governments all over the world needed rope for the war, so the demand far outstripped the supply. Since America's hemp industry was in a shambles as a result of the dope prohibition, they were in a bit of a pickle. Careers had been built ensuring that Americans didn't have access to cannabis plants. But now, when they needed cannabis plants to fight a war, they couldn't very well tell farmers to plant dope in the American heartland!

Or could they? Marijuana was illegal, but it still wasn't common knowledge that hemp and marijuana were the same thing. So some bureaucrat, who probably never connected hemp to marijuana, allocated some of his propaganda budget to tell farmers about the virtues of growing cannabis plants. *Hemp for Victory* is a short propaganda film made in 1942. In it, American farmers are encouraged to do their patriotic duty and grow hemp, for victory. The film extols the virtues of this remarkable plant which can be made into the finest fabric, rope and oil, and will mean jobs at home and victory over the horrible enemy over there. Growing hemp became a patriotic act. Farmers across the country planted hemp seed and supplied the military with the long, strong fibers needed for the war effort. *Hemp For Victory* was a big success.

When the war ended, so did the demand for hemp. Without the Japanese blocking the supply of rope from the Far East, where it could be bought for a song, demand for American-grown hemp dried up. So farmers went back to planting corn for whiskey and tobacco for cigarettes. But they couldn't get rid of the pesky cannabis plants. Plow and sow as much as they liked, there were always patches of that darned hemp growing at the edges of the fields, and on the riverbanks. The film disappeared into the dustbins of history, and nobody thought about it for many years.

Many years later, when America's demand for cannabis plants escalated again, the United States government had forgotten about *Hemp For Victory* and the virtues of cannabis. Cannabis had again become Public Enemy Number One, and the only demand came from beatnik enthusiasts, not admirals and quartermasters. And no government department would want to be connected with extolling the virtues of Public Enemy Number One.

But there was this pesky little film making the rounds of bohemian America. Hipsters roared with laughter at the campy call for America to grow pot. Something had to be done!

And it seems as though something was done. Don't expect to find *Hemp For Victory* at your corner video store. Unless you live down the road from the Library of Congress, and even if you live there, you will be hard pressed to find it. In fact, nearly all record of the film has mysteriously evaporated.

CODA: The Emperor Wore Hemp

Jack Herer is a hemp enthusiast. He is the author of *The Emperor Wears No Clothes,* one of the finest books on the history and future of hemp. He had seen and had a laugh over *Hemp For Victory,* and was intrigued that nobody seemed to know exactly who made it and why. So he started asking.

Nobody seemed to know who made the film. So he kept on asking; letters and phone calls turned up the same results: nothing. Nobody wanted to take the rap for having made a film about growing the evil weed, *Cannabis sativa.* Even the Library of Congress, the figurative Wizard of Oz of American historical authority, had no record of the vile flick. But since the film existed, and was paid for with government funds, the Library of Congress should have a record of it. It's their job. But the Wizard had no record of a film about growing dope in Kansas.

If you are old enough to know about Dorothy and Toto and their whirlwind tour of Kansas, you will remember when libraries had card catalogs. They were long banks of little drawers full of 3 x 5 cards. Over the last 30 years, these cards have been replaced by electromagnetic data files. Many card catalogs have been destroyed, and others removed to storage and forgotten. The Library of Congress is one of those few libraries that have not destroyed their card catalog. The old drawers have been relegated to the historical dustbin, but they are still intact.

And that's where Jack Herer and his friends came up with the dope on *Hemp For Victory.* The electromagnetic data files all over Washington contained no record of the United States Department of Agriculture propaganda department having made the film in 1942, but when the dogged researcher smooth-talked himself into a romp through the forgotten card catalog, *Victory* was his.

Ganja would play an important part in another war, many years later. In the meantime, it continued to thrive on the outskirts of towns like Lawrence, Kansas, and Lansing, Michigan. It just comes up, year after year and makes a pest of itself in ditches and cornfields all over the country. It's still growing wild in most states of union. Whether through ignorance, ineptitude, or fluke, *Hemp For Victory* ensured the viability of cannabis plants in America. More than 25 years after the making of the film, the cannabis fields it nurtured would come back to haunt the drug warriors.

Operation Inept

Operation Intercept was a great idea. It was Nixon's response to the pot-smoking flower children of the 1960's; it was known as his "grass curtain." The idea was to make marijuana from Mexico unavailable to Americans so that they would stop smoking it. Sometimes ideas should remain just that; Operation Intercept is a case in point. For the hippies, it was short-term pain for long-term gain, but from the point of view of the drug warriors, Operation Intercept was a gaff of epic proportions. This blunder will go down as one of the chief reasons America lost the War on Drugs.

In the late 1960's, most of the grass smoked at campus sit-ins and rock concerts originated in Mexico. It was cheap, readily available and reasonably potent. The prohibition kept the price high enough that anybody with the intestinal fortitude could buy a brick of pot in Tijuana for 15 or 20 dollars and sell it back home in America for 20 times that price. So a lot of people bought bricks in Mexico, sweated the customs inspection, and turned a tidy profit in Berkeley, or Detroit, or Lawrence, Kansas. One run across the border in Daddy's new Ford could be worth seven or eight thousand dollars — the price of three new Fords.

Some of these kids took trucks, busses, even private planes, and smuggled bales of boo into the land of the free. Organized crime certainly had a hand in the business, but it was mostly being smuggled by young fortune seekers from the suburbs and colleges.

In 1969, Mexico had a bad spring crop; it rained too much during harvest, and they couldn't get the grass dry before it began to rot. So that summer there was a shortage of grass all over America. The grass shortage didn't make headlines, but everybody felt it; the prices went up, and it was harder to find. Even the narcs knew that there was a shortage of Mexican weed. They were picking up more LSD, peyote, heroin and homegrown marijuana. Maybe this gave them the idea that if they dried up the supply of grass from Mexico permanently, they would be rid of the marijuana problem once and for all. This seems to be what was behind the thinking of Richard Nixon's "Operation Intercept."

On September 21, 1969, just in time for the delivery of Mexico's fall crop, the United States sealed their southern border. Nobody got in without a thorough inspection. Operation Intercept was on. For the next 20 days America could sleep soundly in the knowledge that no marijuana would cross the border by land or sea or air. Radar had been installed, gunboats borrowed from the defense department, and marines patrolled Texas back country roadways. Millions of travelers were detained and questioned; hundreds of thousands were searched; customs officers and treasury police worked overtime to keep the evil weed from creeping north. And it was working. Anybody would have been crazy to try to bring grass across the Mexican border with all this going on. The drought was being felt plenty in Lawrence, and Des Moines, and Lansing, where everybody was counting on the new crop in late September.

So They Made a Hash of it

The American people have a well-earned reputation for ingenuity. If Uncle Sam wouldn't let them bring grass in from Mexico anymore, then they would have to either get it somewhere else, or grow their own. And so they did both. The traditional trickle of hashish from the Near East swelled to a flood of cannabis resin cakes floating in from Lebanon, Turkey, Kashmir, and Morocco. Travelling Americans took the midnight express across the Near East and came back with slabs of hash and contacts for the future.

∘∘∘ *Strange Interlude* ∘∘∘

Midnight Express

The movement of cannabis around the global village got a shot in the arm in the summer of '69, as this tale attests. The story was told to me by a friend of mine, Joe McQuaid, and he assures me that it is absolutely gospel truth. You can believe it or not, as you choose, but either way, it is a remarkable story.

"When I was in high school, you could buy any mind altering drug you had ever heard of without having to leave the neighborhood. To get grass, or acid, or mushrooms, or mescaline, you could either go to the school—more precisely, to the smoking area next to the cafeteria—or you could go to the shopping plaza in the evening. One fine spring day, in the smoking area, a guy I knew, Marty Ouellette, showed up with a chunk of hash to peddle.

"Hash was available in just about every color and country of origin imaginable, because hippies and travelers and budding businessmen were sending it from all over Asia minor and India, so Marty's stash didn't seem in any way unusual. He put some in a pipe for me, hoping I'd either buy some or tell my friends that it was good. And it was. So good, as I remember it, that I convinced my brother George and his friends to pool up their money to buy a slab of it at a bulk-rated price. It was indeed priceless hashish, and I stashed my own chunk away for Christmas. But it was a sad Christmas that year, as our elder brother, Victor, died in Goa, India, that fall.

"Marty Ouellette lived with Paul Vinelander at Rochdale College, in

Toronto. Paul was a bootlegger while at Rochdale and today practices gynecology at a suburban Canadian hospital. Rochdale College was an experimental college which evolved into 'Drug Central' for Canada, and Marty was on the outskirts of the trade. He was a small-timer. He had a little basket that he would lower out his fourth-story window and people wanting to buy or sell contraband could send or receive samples in the basket. One night, Marty told me, a guy came with this Indian hash. He sent up a chunk for inspection. It was very finely hand pressed red hashish that smelled like something out of *One Thousand And One Arabian Nights*. Marty bought all the guy had: nearly three pounds. The next day, he hitchhiked to Windsor to visit his mother, and he brought the block of red hash with him, figuring, rightly, that he could get rid of it at the high schools. Windsor, a veritable suburb of Detroit, enjoyed a well-oiled pipeline for contraband goods, and local kids had a nose for fine hashish. If it smelled like cinnamon, you could sell it in Windsor.

"My brother George and I, and our friends, relieved him of a big slab of it, and I, packrat that I am, kept a diminishing supply of the now infamous Red Indian Hash for several Christmases running. To this day, my brother George still expects me to produce Red Indian Hash at Christmas.

"Many years later, I had dinner with an old family friend. Kyle was a soul mate of my brother, Victor, who I lost to that Summer of Love. Kyle and I were picking tofu out of our teeth in front of a cheery fire in midtown Toronto, when he told me the story of my brother Victor's last adventure. 'You know, there's money in a bank somewhere in Bombay that your brother never collected,' he smiled. 'I sent him two thousand dollars in the late summer, and as far as I know he never went back to Bombay before he died. So there's a couple of thousand dollars sitting, waiting to be collected.'

"I was intrigued by the prospect of money and prodded him for more information. 'In the winter, before he died, he wrote to me telling me that he was going up to Nepal to pony back a big bag of unprocessed hashish resin. I wrote back that I would sell it for him. He could live for a year or two on the money he'd make. So off he went to Nepal, and bought this bag of hash powder. He carted it back to Goa, where he rubbed and pounded it into slabs. He carved the pages out of a book and sent it to me in at my house in Kensington market. So I got this package in the mail, and I let it sit by the door for a month, and then I opened it. The smell was enough to bring an elephant to its knees! Three fat red slabs of finely worked high country hash. I would have kept it, if I could have afforded it. But I broke off a big chunk for myself and took the rest over to Rochdale to sell.' He poured us a fresh glass of wine, and I leaned in for the story. 'So there was this guy at Rochdale, he had a basket on a clothes line, and he sent down the basket, and I sent up a chunk, and he sent down a basket full of twenty dollar bills and I put most of the hash in the basket. So I sent the money along to your brother in Bombay, and it's probably still there.'

"I was, and continue to be, flabbergasted.

"Now, I have never pursued the money, but I have long treasured the curious conspiracy of events which caused me to buy an ounce of finely made hashish that my brother had bought raw in Nepal, hauled back to Goa, sat on the beach and pounded, sent to his friend in Toronto, and had delivered to me and my brother, George, at my school in Windsor at the approximate time of his death.

"Heraclites said that all things conspire, and I am inclined to believe him."

◊ ◊ ◊

At the Quartermaster's Store

The dopers also held the Vietnam card: while Operation Intercept was in full grunt, there was no shortage of weed in the jungle. Bulging parcels arrived at the homes of entrepreneurial war vets across the country; and this was no Mexican home-grown, this was *jungle jive*. When troop ships arrived from the war zone, soldiers came in with sacks of the stuff, and they had an eager market to take it off their hands. No one has ever suggested that America lost the Vietnam War because of grass, but some old vets I know argue that America lost the war on drugs because of Vietnam.

Hemp For Victory, Reprise

Far from the Mexican border and the southeast Asian jungles, the long-dead hemp industry had left patches of tenacious weed all over the country. In the 1940's, *Hemp For Victory* encouraged growers to plant hemp seed, and 25 years later, farmers just couldn't get rid of this Indian hemp that sprouted on the outskirts of their fields. Some of this cannabis was as potent as the Mexican marijuana Americans were used to. And so entrepreneurial hippies and farm boys harvested the local vegetation and smoked their brains out. The cops in places like Lawrence, Kansas, and Omaha, Nebraska, had a fiesta, arresting out-of-state hippies in the old hemp fields back home:

> Now, last year was the first year that we had a great deal of experience with marijuana harvesters coming in from out of State. In the year of 1968, we documented 40 arrests for harvesting marijuana. These were all people from out of State.
>
> To date in 1969 we have documented 81 arrests of people from outside of Nebraska who have come in to harvest the marijuana that is growing here. This represents over a 100-percent increase over last year. ... By coming to Nebraska they eliminate the dangers of crossing an international border ...

> —*Officer W.F. Rowe*
> *Nebraska State Highway Patrol*[1]

Once these fellows got the notion that American soil and American economics was suitable for pot farming, there was no stopping them. With a little tinkering with the soil and a little cross pollination, American dope could rank with the best stuff on the planet. Today's super-strains are the children of Operation Intercept. And Richard Nixon was the fertilizer.

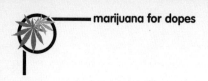
Flight School for Drug Runners

Back in Mexico, there were warehouses full of the fall's bumper crop, and the borders were closed. There were no gringos with yawning trunks to fill with bricks of loco weed. Some of the Mexican dope dealers got desperate and tried their luck against the Texas Rangers and desert radar systems — and they made it! All the king's horses and all the king's men couldn't find a Cessna 140 coming in along the Sierra Madres with a bellyful of contraband. With bigger planes, the sons of Pancho Villa were able to land fifty to a hundred thousand dollars' worth of grass on a single flight. The business was so lucrative that one good run would buy two more planes for next time. Operation Intercept was like a flight school for drug runners. Once the Colombians got involved, the whole industry ratcheted up a notch: It was too lucrative a business to be run by school kids and weekend criminals. Organized crime syndicates took over the marijuana trade.

Intercept What ... in Particular?

On the front lines of Operation Intercept, they weren't exactly making headlines. The army of customs stiffs had stopped the dope from coming in over land, but they hadn't arrested very many bad guys. The amount of grass they were busting was just about the same amount they were finding *without* Operation Intercept. They were getting headlines in Mexico, though: "Mexico Humiliated" roared *La Prensa*. "Unfriendly Behavior" roared the Mexican president. The US National Confederation of Chambers of Commerce called Operation Intercept "an absurd and exaggerated program for the meager results it has produced."[2]

After 20 days of this farce, Nixon withdrew his forces and declared victory. Sound familiar? Operation Intercept packed up its circus — radar, speed boats, and overtime allowances — and went home. The customs officers were said to be too sick and humiliated to talk about it. This is a strange sort of victory, where the victor is too humiliated to brag. But it was certainly a victory for the Americans who like smoking grass. Operation Intercept fostered many new ways for citizens to get a hold of the stuff.

Shotgun

A lot of the Vietnam vets I know say that they would have gone ga-ga in the jungle if they hadn't smoked grass. Most of them don't talk about their 'Nam days much. When they do, they sometimes tell grass stories. Buying it, smoking it, being high under fire — they're good stories. Grass was as big a part of the war in Vietnam as it was at home among us long-haired resistors and detractors. While narcs patroled schoolyards in Kansas looking for nickel bags of Mexican leaf and smoldering draft cards, in Vietnam, anybody but the Military Police could have told you where to score pot. Grass was dirt cheap and as easy to get as booze, and everybody knew it. In Kansas or Michigan or California, it was the same thing: everybody but the cops could get just about anything they wanted. And a lot of people wanted marijuana. For the first time in an American war, booze wasn't the go-to drug of choice. Yankees did the Shotgun.

The American forces in Vietnam were mostly high school grads and drop outs who were not killing and dying willingly. When a fellow's number came up, he had two choices: He could either report or resist. If he resisted, he could go to Canada, or go underground, or go to jail. A lot went to Canada, but many more reported for duty and found themselves squatting in a jungle carrying a rifle or a stretcher.

The ones who came to Canada, or went underground in the US, didn't sit idly by while their school chums killed and died in the jungle; they joined other resistors, angry vets, and high-minded activists in demonstrations against the war. The draft resistors were drawn to the same low-rent neighborhoods as the local hippies, and found that they had much in common. They hated the war, listened to the Stones, and smoked grass as often as possible. They gathered in Stanley Park in Vancouver, and on Yorkville in Toronto to make speeches, smoke dope, and listen to music. There may have been demonstrations against the Vietnam War at which nobody smoked dope, but I never heard of any.

Strange Interlude

Prisoners of War — Children of Peace

A friend of mine, Dick Lowden, did time in 'Nam, and he likes to tell this story. Dick got a bellyful of hard reality in villages near the North border. He is a Kansas boy, and had never heard of marijuana. When the government called, he put on a uniform and did what he was told. One thing he was told, while on patrol in the jungle, was that patrol was safer if he smoked a joint before going out. His sergeant told him he could hear better, see farther and face death more bravely if he smoked some. So he did. You and I might doubt it, but Dick insists that smoking dope saved his life on more than one occasion. If you sit with him long enough, he might tell you stories of being stoned under fire. Dick learned to like smoking grass, and he still smokes it at every reasonable opportunity.

When he came home to Kansas in '67 Dick bought his grass from other vets who had connections. They had it shipped in by buddies in southeast Asia. One clear June night, the night of his kid brother's high school graduation, Dick sneaked out behind the barn to have a quiet toke where nobody would find him. He was a proud vet and had attended the ceremonies fully dressed, and he was still in uniform. As he came around the back of the barn, ready to spark up, he found his kid brother and his buddies smokin' a reefer. They ditched the doobie in a hurry when big brother came along the trail, but the tell-tale smell and guilty, glassy eyes were unmistakable. "We never smoked it before, honest," one of the kids, the Wagner boy, confessed. "We'll never smoke it again."

Dick puts his official face on for this part of the story. His eyes bug out as he snaps to attention. "Bull shit," he says to the kid. "While I'm over there, risking my butt for you little dirt balls, you're out behind the barn breaking federal laws." Dick will tell you how the kid looked when he barked him to attention, and his eyes bug out even further. "The least you can do when smoking mary-ji-wanna in the presence of a United States soldier," Dick was nose to nose with the petrified senior, "is to offer him a toke!"

Dick forces a laugh at this point in his bittersweet story. In 1967, a high school graduation party was a going away party, too. Unless a kid had marks to get a scholarship, graduation meant draft eligibility, and Uncle Sam needed help. Some of these boys, the Wagner boy among them, would be in boot camp before harvest festival. Dick lit up a fat, smelly joint of Kampuchean Highlander. Kampuchean cannabis was probably available to soldiers in Vietnam, but stateside, nobody got anything much stronger than Acapulco gold — unless your good buddy in the next town was a quartermaster in 'Nam and could still get shipments of the world's finest exotica. Dick likes to brag about the quality of the boo back in those heady days before high tech "bud" was invented. In his words: "This Kampuchean Highlander was the highest shit this side of heaven. You know what? Them buggers had the ride of their lives under that sparkling June moon…" Two of them, Wagner and one other kid, Dick will tell you, when you have finished smiling over the story, did have the ride of their lives. The last ride. They reported for duty, and were dead before Christmas.

◊ ◊ ◊

Ganja 101

On campus, grass was a badge. It said, "I don't buy into the status quo." It was probably unwelcome in engineering schools and medical faculties, but it made for very lively debate in psychology and physics classes. Students did a lot of sitting-in in the 1960's, and while they were sitting, they were usually smoking pot. If your mother went to college in the 60's, or 70's, she probably smoked pot. If she went to anti-war demonstrations or Rolling Stones concerts, then she almost certainly smoked pot. If she still has an earring with a feather on one end and a roach clip on the other, then the jury is in.

The coalition of the anti-war communities and the hippies take some due credit for speeding the end of the Vietnam era. But they too had their wounds and subjects on which they were silent. Most of the hippies I knew became lawyers, teachers, accordion players, psychologists, and local politicians, and the only subject they are silent about is grass. A lot of them still smoke it, but they don't tell their kids.

The War Begins for Real

In 1976, fed up with the marijuana problem, President Gerald Ford brought out the big guns. Sixty million dollars were allocated to a program to spray the Mexican marijuana fields with deadly poison.

Paraquat is a non-selective herbicide that causes plants to wither and die. It does about the same thing to people who ingest enough of it. The effects of paraquat poisoning in humans include irreversible lung damage, kidney failure, and death. Millions of dollars were spent in the effort to eradicate the grass at the source. Of course, the marijuana growers were criminals who didn't care whether the dope was poison or not; they baled it up and shipped it north regardless of its potential danger.

Now, it's not as though the authorities were ignorant of the health consequences of smoking paraquat-laced pot. They knew full well what the consequences of the policy would be, and they decided that the only good American pot smoker was a diseased or dead American pot smoker. Georgia governor Joe Harris said, "We don't have any responsibility to those people. They are breaking the law."[3]

The problem for these tokers was that they couldn't tell which dope was sprayed and which was not. Those who had a hankering for altering their consciousness either took the gamble that they had clean pot, or they chose a less risky route to inebriation, like speed, or LSD, or heroin, or cocaine. The Reagan administration's chief drug advisor, Carlton Turner, assured the nation that paraquat poisoning was a just punishment for kids who chose to break the law. And he should have known, since his last job had involved selling paraquat test kits through mail-order marijuana magazines.

There was a time when the American government argued it had prohibited marijuana because it was a health risk. Once the paraquat poisoning program was unveiled, they could no longer sustain that sort of logic. Marijuana smoking had become such a heinous crime against humanity that smokers deserved disability or death. Exactly why marijuana smoking is deserving of the death penalty is a question well worth debating, but in lieu of such a debate, we see the continued use of paraquat and related herbicides.

The Peanut Butter Peace Sign

Under the Carter presidency, the War on Drugs took a brief holiday. Jimmy Carter's drug policy began with a very different approach to the control of mind-altering substances. He actually wanted to educate Americans on the dangers of a wide range of psychoactive substances, including marijuana, tobacco, alcohol, and coffee. For Carter, these drugs were all part of a continuum, and to criminalize users of some and promote the use of others endangered the health of the American people and the credibility of their government. In fact, Jimmy Carter proposed the radical idea that the marijuana laws should not cause more harm than marijuana itself, and he attempted to turn this revolutionary idea into law.

The Carter approach to the marijuana problem included decriminalization of possession of small amounts of the drug, putting a stop to spraying poison on cannabis fields, and funding a program of drug education and rehabilitation. These ideas were supported by such radical liberals as the American Bar Association, the American Medical Association, and the American Council of Churches.

The US House of Representatives didn't look very favorably on these fanatical ideas, and they let the proposed legislation die on the order paper.

After all, how could America back out of another war? They hadn't yet recovered their pride after losing a president to impeachment and a war to the North Vietnamese; they were not about to let a bunch of bleeding-heart liberals direct the course of American morality.

When Carter's main drug policy advisor, Peter Bourne, was accused of using cocaine at a party hosted by NORML, and was charged with writing a bogus prescription for one of his aides, the wheels fell off the new "harm reduction" model of drug abuse legislation, and the drug warriors were back in control. During the Carter years, a few states lowered the penalties for possession of pot, but very little changed in America's attitude concerning cannabis flowers.

Ray Gun

When Ronald Reagan came to power in 1981, he left no doubt about which side of the drug war he supported. Drugs were Public Enemy Number One again. No distinction was made between cannabis and cocaine; all recreational drugs, except for the legal ones, were the enemies of America, and so were their users.

> We're rejecting the helpless attitude that drug use is so rampant that we're defenseless to do anything about it. We're taking down the surrender flag that has flown over so many drug efforts. We're running up the battle flag. We can fight the drug problem, and we can win.
>
> —*Ronald Reagan*[4]

In a frenzied assault on the American drug culture, Reagan raised the federal law enforcement budget from Carter's measly $850 million to nearly $7 billion dollars. He called out the military. He called out the media. *He called out the First Lady!* America no longer tolerated casual use of illegal substances. Pot smokers were told to just say no.

If you were the type who just couldn't say no, you might go to one of the new prisons they built to hold all the pot smokers. America incarcerates more of its citizens than any country in the world. Sixty percent of these prisoners are in jail for drug-related crimes, and nearly thirty percent of the drug offenders are in prison for having marijuana. Once in prison, a citizen generally has access to as much marijuana, heroin, barbiturates, and other contraband as he can handle, but even then, he should just say "No."

In the Reagan era, the grass sold in prison or at the local tavern might have been laced with deadly poison. Spraying paraquat on cannabis intended for American distribution made a big comeback under Ronald Reagan. But this time Reagan didn't just spray the stuff on Mexican hemp fields, he sprayed it on the US National Forests in order to convince the Colombian government that America was committed to the drug war!

Reagan managed to strong-arm a change in the Posse Comitatus Act, allowing, for the first time in over one hundred years, the allocation of military personnel and equipment in the enforcement of civilian laws. The Navy was used to train and support the Coast Guard, the Army and Marines were pressed into service, and the Air Force had regular patrols over known and suspected drug routes. All the king's horses and all the king's men were out to get all users of illegal drugs.

All this activity drove the price of marijuana from about $50 an ounce to about $150 an ounce. Meanwhile, the price of hard drugs like heroin and cocaine had dropped off just as radically. With all these interdiction efforts, it became too risky to ship bulky agricultural products across the fortified border; it was much simpler and more profitable to import heroin and cocaine. Organized crime doesn't care much what the consequences of their activities involve, their job is to make money. And they were very definitely making money.

The man behind the Reagan drug agenda became America's next president, and Vice President George Bush knew a lot about the drug trade. He had been involved with it for most of his professional career. George Bush was a career drug czar. There are people who believe that George Bush and

Oliver North were dealing on both sides of the drug war, and many interesting books and articles have been published on the subject.[5] Whatever one believes about their role, it is clear that George Bush knew the drug industry inside out. Heck, under George Bush, the price of marijuana went from 150 dollars an ounce to nearly 400 dollars; and to achieve this marvel he increased the interdiction cost from seven billion dollars to more than twelve billion.

War on Overdrive

In the early '80's, everybody in the drug industry was making money. There were jobs for nickel-bag runners, prosecutors, jail guards, chemists, cops, file clerks, pilots, mules, and lobbyists. The drug business became bigger than legitimate big business, and its invisibility and tax-free status made it very attractive to those who wanted to finance freedom fighters, or governments, or mercenary armies.

The ranks of officers and foot soldiers swelled beyond anything since the days of the Roman Empire. Tens of thousands of government employees were engaged in the pursuit of drug users, sellers, growers, and importers. More money was being spent on drug interdiction than on almost any other single government activity. But while all the king's horses were rounding up small-time losers and casual users, vast fortunes were accumulating in the criminal underworld, and there were more drugs than ever. George Bush's armies couldn't keep contraband out of American noses, forearms, and lungs. The price of pot went through the roof, but the cost of heroin and cocaine actually decreased, due to the oversupply.

When George Bush left office, the street price of an ounce of marijuana reached the high-water mark of about $450, and the Federal Drug Control budget peaked at nearly $13,000,000,000 (that's $13 billion). Nobody knows how much grass Americans smoke, since most Americans don't broadcast their casual drug use, but conservative estimates from the George Bush era range between two and five tons per day. If they smoked two-and-a-half tons per day, the marijuana business was worth something like $43 million dollars per day, or about $15 billion annually — about the same amount as the American people were spending trying to prohibit it.

The One Person Who Didn't Inhale

Bill Clinton's administration will be remembered less for his stand on drugs, which was described by his opponents as soft, and more for his wandering willie, which nobody described as soft. His credibility was further softened by his admission to having tried marijuana. He tried it, didn't like it, and didn't inhale, or so he said.

Clinton is probably not the first president to have smoked cannabis flowers. George Washington is at the top of the suspect list, followed by Thomas Jefferson, both of whom grew the stuff. Nobody would suggest that Washington, Jefferson, Madison, Monroe, Jackson, Taylor or Pierce, or Benjamin Franklin were dope fiends, but there does seem to be evidence that the Fathers of America were aware of the psychoactive benefits of the hemp plant. "Pierce, Taylor and Jackson, all military men, smoked it with their troops. Cannabis was twice as popular among American soldiers in the Mexican War as in Vietnam: Pierce wrote to his family that it was 'the only good thing' about the war."[6]

With the arrival of the Democrats in the White House in 1993, it became clear that the king's horses had taken control of the drug policy agenda. Bill Clinton came to power intending to shift the focus of the drug war from an enforcement model to a treatment model. He framed his approach as "tough but smart."

It didn't require a rocket scientist to see that America was losing the War on Drugs. There was more money being spent on police, prisons, and courts than ever before, and there were more drugs available than ever before. The Democrats said that they would do things differently:

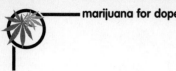

Insanity is doing the same old thing over and over again and expecting a different result.

—Bill Clinton
Campaign debate, October 11, 1992

Clinton had a good mentor. A rocket scientist, in fact:

Insanity [is] ... continuing to do the same things and expecting different results.

—Albert Einstein

But the United States government is not overrun by rocket scientists, and they insist on doing the same old thing. Clinton proposed to change the focus from incarceration of addicts and users to treatment for addicts and users. He didn't ever seriously propose anything so radical as the decriminalization of hemp farming or marijuana smoking, but he did intend to spend more of the drug war money on medical approaches and psychological treatment centers. However, these proposals were interpreted as "soft on drugs," and soundly trashed in committee and Congress. Exactly why the American legislators cannot seriously consider a change in the failed prohibition is a moot point. A cynic might suggest that too many people are making too much money to allow the trough to be turned over to health care and social workers, but a more generous view suggests that the policies are well intended but misguided.

There is no sign that the United States government will give up on the drug war any time soon. It does not matter that courts have found the prohibition of cannabis flowers to be a gross intrusion on citizens' rights, or that every relevant study has called for their decriminalization, or even that tens of millions of otherwise law-abiding Americans smoke the stuff — the prohibition of marijuana has become a religion.

From kindergarten, Americans are taught about the evils of cannabis. Pamphlets are handed out, police officers visit classrooms and show videotapes, and huge sums have been spent on Internet sites. And yet, every day, millions of Americans smoke marijuana.

Bad guys smoke it. But so do cops, and hairdressers, prosecuting attorneys, Olympic medallists, grave diggers, insurance office clerks, and publishers. Only you don't see these people in handcuffs very often. Instead of handcuffs, they have surprise urine tests. And they can buy test kits and cleansing agents that will ensure their urine is clear of marijuana, or cocaine, or heroin, so that they can keep their jobs. And many of these people support the War on Drugs.

Franz Kafka Would Be Proud

Since before its prohibition, Americans have enjoyed smoking cannabis, but it was a pleasure known to very few. When prohibition was introduced, the value of marijuana rose to a level that made selling it a profitable trade. Initially use was confined to the margins of society. Through the 1950's and 60's, smoking pot became entrenched in American society. Kerouac and Ginsberg did not create a generation of addicts and idlers, but rather they contributed to the generation that stopped the Vietnam War and today runs the White House.

The demand for marijuana at every level of society created a supply system that by definition was criminal, but was largely run by non-violent, small-time adventurers. As the scale of prohibition enforcement increased, so did the value of the commodity, which became of great interest to more hardened criminal syndicates. As the twenty-first century rushes in, more Americans smoke cannabis than ever before.

They do it quietly, though, or they do it in jail. In America today, most people who go to jail for marijuana are poor people. If judges get caught with cannabis metabolites in their urine, they suffer the disfavor of their peers, and probably a return to private practice. If a kid gets nabbed a couple of times for selling nickel bags in the washroom, he suffers incarceration with rapists and murderers. And once in jail, he has access to virtually every vice known to humankind. The drug war is a real war. There are many casualties.

There have been, and probably will continue to be, changes in the laws regarding the use of cannabis in medicine. Across the Americas, doctors and patients are insisting on the right to use marijuana in the treatment of disease. And they are winning. Cannabis buyers' clubs are tolerated or legal in many states of the union. Even the United States government, however reluctantly, provides marijuana, free of charge, to a few of its citizens.

The marijuana-growing industry was a direct consequence of the War on Drugs. Americans might have been quite happy to go on smoking Mexican leaf and seed were it not for Richard Nixon's Operation Intercept, but today the industry is broad, deep, and lucrative. High-quality American weed is worth up to five thousand dollars a pound to a grower. On any one acre of America's four billion acres, a farmer can produce up to a million dollars' worth of herb, sometimes twice a year. And for doing so, he could wind up in a federal prison for life.

The place of marijuana in American society is nothing if not peculiar.

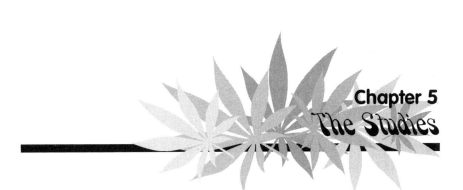

Chapter 5
The Studies

EVERY TIME SOMEBODY SUGGESTS REFORMING THE LAWS PROHIBITING GRASS, somebody else says that we don't know enough about it and there ought to be a study commissioned. They've been at this business for a hundred years, and the vast majority of the reports agree that there is very little to get excited about. While many investigators have called for the regulation of cannabis distribution, virtually all of the studies agree that prohibition causes more harm to society than grass ever could ever hope to. Yet, excepting a few notable jurisdictions, very little progress has been made in bringing the law into line with the recommendations of our advisors. Every major study in the English language agrees that prohibition is neither morally justifiable nor socially practicable. And yet people are still jailed for smoking the stuff.

The Indian Hemp Drugs Commission

The first report of consequence in modern times was commissioned by the British government in 1892. The British ruled India, and as the smoking and eating of cannabis products was unfamiliar to the conquering nation, they naturally regarded it as a potential problem. How do the British solve a problem? They set out a committee of bearded fellows to investigate. The Indian Hemp Drugs Commission was charged with investigating the use of cannabis as a euphoric among the people of India. They interviewed many hundreds of Indians and British subjects across the sub-continent and brought forth a 3,281-page report. Having studied the problem from stem to stern, they concluded that "moderate use of these drugs is the rule, and that the excessive use is comparatively exceptional. The moderate use produces practically no ill effects."

The use of the herb for social and religious customs was so pervasive and the excessive or harmful use so infrequent that the commission regarded the prohibition of the drugs as unwarranted and ill advised. Depriving people of a substance they enjoyed and was deeply ingrained in the cultural life of India would have been a gross intrusion into the society and customs of their "hosts." They thought it would be better to tax the purchase of bhang, thereby ameliorating the excessive use of the drug, and filling their coffers at one and the same time. The Brits are nothing if not practical.

Soldiers' Joy:
The Panama Canal Zone Reports

When reports of soldiers smoking up behind the barracks in the Panama Canal Zone surfaced, the top brass took action. They thought very carefully about it and decided to prohibit the use of marijuana and to commission a study of the situation. The year was 1916, and the soldiers were American. Pot smoking caught on among the weary functionaries of the American presence in Central America. There wasn't much to do except stand outside a hut with a rifle on your shoulder or polish your boots, and smoking the local loco weed hardly impaired a soldier's ability to carry out these tasks.

The members of the first Panama Canal Zone Commission were thorough: they even smoked some themselves to see what all the fuss was about.

The red-eyed doctors and captains concluded that the resulting intoxication was nothing to be alarmed about. Smoking marijuana would not affect the performance of their personnel any more than alcohol, which was not prohibited except while on duty, so the commission's report in 1925 recommended that nothing should be done about smoking dope out behind the barracks. While they did recommend a "no smoking dope while on duty" policy they recommended against an outright ban. The prohibition was off.

Nevertheless, the senior brass didn't like it. They ordered a new commission in 1929. This one concluded that "use of the drug is not widespread and ... its effects upon military efficiency and upon discipline are not great. There appears to be no reason for renewing the penalties formerly exacted for the possession and the use of the drug."

So what did the military do? They renewed the prohibition. They put dopers in the lock-up and commissioned another study. The final committee, deployed in 1931, combed through all the documentation on marijuana, conducted dozens of personal interviews, and reported honestly. They concluded that there was indeed a significant problem with delinquency and psychopathic behavior among the occupying forces in the Canal Zone, but that this was due, not to marijuana, but to the fact that "a large proportion of the delinquents are morons or psychopaths, which conditions themselves would serve to account for delinquency."

The solution to the problem was obvious — which is, perhaps, why the United States government missed it. They once again renewed the prohibition of marijuana in the Canal Zone.

The Classic: La Guardia

The next major study was not conducted, as one might imagine, prior to the imposition of cannabis prohibition in the United States, but some seven years later in 1944, when New York mayor Fiorello La Guardia, fed up with spending money rounding up pot-smoking "negroes and hindoos," commissioned a study of the marijuana habit in New York City.

The La Guardia Commission Report is regarded as one of the most thorough studies in its field. Thousands of years of social, legal and medical literature was consulted and digested. They concluded that there was very little to get excited about. Cannabis users should be left alone. "The practice of smoking marihuana does not lead to addiction in the medical sense of the word … the publicity concerning the catastrophic effects of marihuana smoking in New York City is unfounded."

Nevertheless, possession of marijuana remained illegal, and little has changed, in spite of the avalanche of scientific confirmation of this report.

Pop Stars and Egg Heads: The Wootten Report

Britain's Wootten Report was just like all the others. It grudgingly concluded that there was really nothing very horrible about smoking grass, and to imprison people for doing so was neither moral nor practical. Some parsimoniously enlightened social policy regarding cannabis prohibition resulted from it, but the most interesting thing about the Wootten Report was the context in which it was conducted and the characters involved.

Baroness Barbara Wootten, a noted social scientist and veteran of the British House of Commons, had sat on many Royal Commissions. In 1966 she was charged with exploring and reporting on the medical and pharmacological properties of cannabis and LSD. Her investigative team included the most eminent medical, pharmacological, psychiatric, and sociological minds of the period. The listing of Ph.D.'s and Emeritus Professorships were enough to fill a page of the final report. Unlike the British Indian Hemp Drug Commissioners of 70 years previous, it was not their role to advise on social policy, but rather to investigate and report on the hard science.

That was before Steve Abrams and the infamous SOMA advertisement appeared. The SOMA advertisement was a public declaration that appeared in the *Times* of London on July 24, 1967. It was signed by some of the foremost intellectual, literary, scholarly, and medical thinkers of the day.

Alongside Sergeant Pepper's four lads, (who ponied up the cost of the advert out of the Lonely Heart's Club album promotion budget), we find names like Francis Crick (the Nobel Prize-winning biophysicist), R.D. Laing (the most controversial psychological thinker since Freud), Graham Greene (the epitome of modern English literature), and Francis Huxley (whose ancestors and anthropological seat at Oxford had given him a fair share of fame and glory). The SOMA advertisement called for the Wootten Commission to investigate the social circumstances and consequences of cannabis consumption, and to make recommendations for the reshaping of social policy. The signatories to the advertisement were an impressive-enough lot to convince the government and the committee to take a good hard look at the legal and social considerations.

Meanwhile, Rolling Stones Mick Jagger and Keith Richards were being dragged through the courts and trashed in the tabloids for being dope-smoking fiends. The police had raided a late-night party at Richards' home where they were caught in the act. Rumors were rife that the Beatles were present the night the Stones were busted, but that the police waited until the four national sweethearts left the party before busting in on Jagger and the bad boys of pop music. Richards was given a year in prison for his part as host of the pot party, and Jagger, as ever, dodged the blow.

Due to the international agreement to prohibit possession of grass, the crime was punishable by imprisonment in Europe as well as in America. But that didn't stop the sons and daughters of the rich and famous on both sides of the Atlantic from gathering in gardens and parading through parks to smoke it and "be in." The year was 1967. The pillars of society and their children found themselves in courtrooms and newspaper scandals for smoking the stuff. There were "be-ins" at Hyde Park. Allen Ginsberg stood on a stump and sang the praises of pot. Flower children were planting themselves around Stonehenge, passing panatellos and dropping acid. There was dancing in the streets.

In this context, faced with flower power in Hyde Park and the Who's Who of the nation ganging up on them, the Wootten Commissioners had little choice. If the people of Britain wanted to know how cannabis functioned in society as well as how it operated in the brain, they would make it their business to find out. The Commission undertook to investigate and report on the social, legal, medical, and pharmacological aspects of cannabis. They were to base their recommendations for law reform on the strength of their research. The genie was out of the bottle.

Two years later, much to the chagrin of the British House of Commons, the Wootten Report appeared as a strongly argued call for the reform of cannabis laws in Britain. The Commissioners didn't exactly approve of cannabis but they felt the iron-fisted prohibition was neither justifiable nor practical. Once again, cannabis was found not guilty of corrupting society.

> Having reviewed all the material available to us we find ourselves in agreement with the conclusions reached by the Indian Hemp Drugs Commission (1893–4) and the New York Mayor's Committee on Marihuana (1944) that 'the long term consumption of cannabis in moderate doses has no harmful effects.'
>
> — *The Wootten Report, section 2*

Once again, the considered opinions of the best minds in the land had very little influence on the law makers. British cannabis smokers continued to face penalties ranging from exorbitant fines to imprisonment.

The Great White North: Canada's Le Dain Commission

Canada is a sober nation where freedom and social order are valued in equal measure. Canadians are not accustomed to seeing their children dancing in the streets. In the late 1960's, the children of the Great White North were dancing in the streets. With flowers in their hair. Giant puppets paraded in Stanley Park and Yorkville was a street party. Canadian kids from Come-by-Chance to Medicine Hat were flocking to the cities to be in the scene. Folk singers and coppers worked overtime entertaining and arresting the teens who tuned in, dropped acid, and smoked dope. Perhaps no one would have been so very alarmed but for the fact that a lot of these kids were being criminalized and incarcerated for the abominable act of smoking grass and having fun.

Canada's new prime minister, Pierre Elliot Trudeau, was the fresh wind of the future. He wore jeans and a leather jacket, and his hair was too long. Trudeau was the man who took the government "out of the bedrooms of the nation," repealing laws against homosexuality and other consensual variations of human relations. He welcomed American draft resisters and had dinner with Castro.

The establishment didn't trust this philosopher king. But in Canada, like everywhere else in the 1960's, the establishment's children were smoking grass and doing time. Something had to be done. Canada couldn't have dancing in the streets and senator's sons in the clink! Trudeau appointed Gerard Le Dain to head up a commission of inquiry. He gave Le Dain bags of money and a broad mandate to investigate and report on the growing non-medical use of drugs in Canada.

The Commission would leave no stone unturned. For the next several years, the commissioners and their attendant squads of graduate students flung themselves into the task, collecting data, conducting experiments, and holding public hearings. They flew around the globe attending and reporting on conferences, talking to police and medical people. They talked to puppeteers in Stanley Park and to folk singers on Yorkville. They talked to psychiatrists at McGill, to prisoners at Kingston Pen and to housewives in suburban Vancouver. They hired students to smoke grass and placeboes in turn, and measured every quantifiable physical and mental indicator. Try as they might, they found very little to get excited about. They found that people who used cannabis were just about like everybody else. Their report is as dry as an old bone. Only the very serious student of scientific inquiry would read every word.

While the Le Dain Commission did not find any grave health or social consequences attached to smoking cannabis, they believed that it was a dele-terious habit and should particularly be avoided by the young. Like tobacco or alcohol, its abuse should be discouraged. While the Commissioners did not all agree on the recommendations for law reform, they agreed on this much: Canadians should not be imprisoned for their enjoyment of cannabis. The Le Dain Commission Reports have been collecting dust since they were issued by the Queen's Printer in 1972.

In Canada, in 1996, a senate commission unanimously recommended ending the pathological practice of incarcerating citizens for smoking cannabis. They recommended a "harm reduction model" fashioned after the Dutch experience. Then they sent this report to the House of Commons.

In 1997, the House of Commons passed the Controlled Substances Act. Under this Act, a citizen is liable to fine and imprisonment for possession of a controlled substance. Controlled substances, under the Act, include "poppy seeds" (my bagel), "Cannabis sativa" (my shirt), and "other sub-stances not listed in tables 1-6" (anything else). If a Canadian puts grow-lights in his closet so that he never has to traffic with criminals or contribute to the underground economy, the Mounties can ride in and confiscate his house as a "fortified drug factory."

The Le Dain Commission was an interesting exercise in social studies, but it had no appreciable effect on the thinking of Canadian law makers.

An American Solution: The Consumers Union Report on Licit and Illicit Drugs

If you've got a problem with your wonky washing machine or your aging automobile, you might begin by kicking it or whacking it with your fist. When this gentle persuasion fails to produce the desired results, you might just get out a sledge hammer or a chain saw.

In the end, many Americans end up at the library, poring over the pages of *Consumer Reports* magazine to find a suitable replacement. Americans trust the Consumers Union reports. In their laboratories and libraries, the

Consumers Union conduct impartial studies of all the available products in a given category and make recommendations for the best products on the market. *Consumer Reports* saves the consumer the hassle and expense of buying a lemon or wielding a sledge hammer.

America has a problem with drugs, licit and illicit. Fixing this problem began with rounding up jazz singers and Mexicans and has escalated into filling up the jails with hundreds of thousands of American citizens. The US government has been flailing about with the sledge hammer now for more than 50 years. The resulting paucity of positive results is frightening. And yet, the War on Drugs continues. They should look at the *Consumers Union Report on Licit and Illicit Drugs.*

The *Consumers Union Report,* which has been readily available at every public library in the nation since 1972, chronicles drug use in America from caffeine to cocaine. In 70 readable chapters, the Consumers Union examines the history, science, and social place of many of America's favorite addictions. They make specific recommendations for the reform of drug laws and policies, and provide lucid and informed argument to back up their proposals. The sledge-hammer approach to cannabis control is not exactly "Highly Recommended" by the report; in fact, Consumers calls for the immediate and complete removal of marijuana from the list of controlled substances. In place of prohibition, they recommend warning labels on every packet of grass, explaining that there may be unknown hazards related to using the product, much like those on a pack of smokes.

At the opening of the 21st century, the American obsession with stamping out marijuana has reached a delirious pitch. Tens of billions of dollars are spent every year finding and jailing citizens who choose to smoke grass. They have once again declared War on Drugs. The costs of this war are staggering, and the outcomes are ominous:

An American citizen flying into Dallas, Texas, was carrying more money than some pimple-faced rookie thought he ought to have on his person. The money was confiscated on the spot for "suspicion of intention to traffic in drugs." Whether this guy ever got his money back is unknown. The story went cold in the press.

In Michigan, a youngster was stopped for speeding and the cop found a roach in the ashtray of his dad's brand new truck. Dad lost the truck, and sonny did thirty days in a county jail cell he shared with rapists and thugs. Pop's truck now belongs to the local constabulary; Sonny may never recover from the experience.

A farmer in Montana lost his house, his vehicle and his freedom for seven years for the crime of telling an undercover police officer, who was posing as a pot buyer, which of his neighbors might have some dope for sale. This man is now in prison. His wife and four children are now fed by the welfare authorities of the state of Montana. The neighbor turned state's evidence and walked away scot-free.

Cases like these can be found with alarming regularity in the pages of newspapers across the western world. These are precisely the outcomes foreseen by the Indian Hemp Drugs Commission more than one hundred years ago. Virtually all of the studies have warned that great harm would ensue from the enforcement of a prohibition of this drug. The price of prohibition is too high. If America is in the market for a new policy, they ought to look it up in *Consumers Reports*.

The Ignored Conclusion — Turn the Page

Clearly, the prohibition of cannabis is not based on the harm that the drug may cause to individuals or to society. While this may once have been offered as the motive for cannabis prohibition, it is no longer a sustainable argument. Study after study has demonstrated that enforcement of the prohibition causes tremendous harm to both society and to individuals. The validation of these studies is starkly available in the daily newspapers, courtrooms and jail houses across the western world. The laws have criminalized huge numbers of citizens, cost untold billions of dollars in enforcement and lost productivity, have warped the integrity of enforcement personnel, and

put the justice system into disrepute. If law makers were concerned about harm to society and individuals, they would declare a war on prohibition.

Perhaps we need a commission to study society's addiction to prohibition. At the very least, we should look elsewhere for an explanation for the continued application of failed social policies.

Chapter 6
The Hemp Business (It's Not What You Think)

OVER THE LAST FEW YEARS, MANY BOOKS ABOUT THE HEMP BUSINESS HAVE appeared in publishers' catalogs. They chronicle a vast array of products and industries that can be fueled by ganja power. From the sheer number of these books about rope and paper, one might reasonably conclude that the business of making money from cannabis is about the manufacture of utilitarian products. Unaccountably, this mundane side of the industry is largely a latent possibility; the hemp business today is not about stems and seeds, it's primarily about cops and robbers.

In the introduction to his very readable study of the economics of marijuana in America, Roger Warner takes us along for a nickel-bag dope deal outside the offices of the Drug Enforcement Agency in Washington, DC. He demonstrates to the DEA that just about any American can buy grass for recreational use any time, anywhere.[7] While this is amusing in itself, it is instructive to visit the introductory pages of Rowan Robinson's 1996 publication, *The Great Book of Hemp*, in which we are told that the book was not printed, as intended, on hemp paper, but on paper made from trees, because hemp paper was unavailable.[8]

The prohibition on cannabis is supposed to be about its euphoric uses, but it is the industrial applications that are effectively suppressed. The juxtaposition of the two introductory passages above illustrates a little-understood fact: The hemp industry is not what you think. It should be about cloth and rope and plastic, but it is almost entirely concerned with law and its enforcement. The lion's share of the cannabis industry today revolves around two related sectors: those involved in the manufacture and distribution of illegal euphoric preparations, and the law enforcement systems that are employed to control them.

In the past, cannabis was put to more productive industrial purposes, including the manufacture of paper, clothes, oils, and foodstuffs. It was responsible for the creation of vast fortunes in legitimate trade. Today, the vast fortunes are enjoyed only by those who organize themselves into criminal syndicates for distribution into the illegal drug market, and by those whose job it is to stem this flow of illicit material.

This should lead us to question the relationship between cannabis and our economy. The question is not whether cannabis is an economic engine, for clearly history and high taxes tell us that it is; the question we have to ask is, what sort of industry do we want hemp to fuel?

> When access to cannabis is restored, a major new branch of the health care and concessions industry will emerge, generating billions of dollars of new capital for the whole economy...[9]

In the United States today, just about anybody who has the inclination to buy a bag of grass can do so without too much trouble. If they are in the habit of doing this, they probably have ready access to fresh, meticulously groomed sinsemilla. No stems, no seeds. The marijuana-growing industry is booming across America, and the products are of a very high quality.

The same is true of the grass growing in the Netherlands, Denmark, Canada, Germany, Switzerland, France, and most other nations under prohibition. The international interdiction of cannabis drugs has done little to stem the consumption of hemp products for recreation. In fact, quite the opposite is true. The artificially high value of the product ensures the health of the illicit industry.

If, however, the publisher of this book wanted to print twenty-five or thirty thousand copies on hemp paper, it would be practically impossible. The paper is available — it is acid-free, stronger, and better lasting by far than this tree-based paper — but it would cost the earth. Hemp paper is currently considered "exotic" in the industry. If you were in the market for a new hemp shirt, or a pair of hemp blue jeans, you could find them, but again, they would be prohibitively expensive. Where can you find hemp-based cosmetics, oil paints, varnishes, or plastics? These products are all available, but they're not easy to locate, and again, they command a premium price. And nobody is getting rich selling these products. So you can buy dope anywhere, but the industrial hemp products are virtually unavailable.

What have all the billions spent on prohibiting grass and locking up citizens really achieved? What benefits has the War on Drugs brought us? It has guaranteed the viability of an illicit market while making the legitimate economics virtually impossible.

The Real Enemy

This may lead you to believe that the War on Drugs is failing, but that depends on what you believe the war is really about. If you own a logging company, or a cotton plantation, or an oil well, you might just think the War on Drugs was working. And those employed in the detection, arrest, defense, prosecution, sentencing, and jailing of joint smokers might just think the War on Drugs was working, too. People who get to confiscate all of the worldly assets of dope smokers think the War on Drugs is great! And let's not forget those fearless entrepreneurs who cash in on the high-value trade in black market pot. Tons of marijuana changes hands daily and fortunes are fattened from New York to Nelson. These people don't think prohibition is so bad.

Grass is responsible for a good deal of money floating around, but the whole industry is non-productive; from bike-gangs to jail guards, it is entirely dependent on the legal prohibition. The international prohibition against cannabis has not prevented, or even stifled, the flow of Acapulco Gold, but it has managed to convert an agricultural and industrial boon into a cauldron of crime and enforcement.

If grass were legal, cannabis deals would go down in hardware stores. If cannabis products were available on a level playing field with other sources of industrial fodder, the impact would be felt from Wall Street to Cali and back again. We know from history that cannabis provides vital fibers, seeds, oils, and medicine. We know that cannabis produces far more useable product per acre than almost any other crop, and that its utility is almost unlimited. The re-introduction of cannabis into the modern, legitimate economy would have an impact on the economics of oil, timber, cotton, building products, pharmaceuticals, clothing and plastics, to name a few.

Dead Weed

Despite this sustained prohibition, the re-introduction of cannabis into the legal market place shows promise worldwide. There is a vibrant and growing constituency throughout the industrial world who are demanding to be able to grow hemp plants that are unfit to smoke. You can grow it in Britain, under special permit, in the Netherlands, where they are less concerned over your THC levels, in France, Spain, Poland, Russia, China, India, even the Canadians are allowing farmers to grow bad dope, with a permit, and a license, and a "security screen."

This is a doper's nightmare: Fields of healthy hemp plants wafting their blunt pollen all over his *ruderalis canadianis* plants and turning them into seeds and stems. Industrial hemp enthusiasts are not interested in *ruderalis canadianis*, unless it's got good seeds and stems.

Bird Feed

Some people think cannabis seeds are for the birds. Well, they are. In fact, when the United States Congress began the prohibition of hemp in 1937, the only exemption to the prohibition was for bird seed manufacturers. They were not allowed to grow hemp, but they were allowed to import as many seeds as they wanted, just so long as they had been de-natured before entering the country.

But seeds aren't just for the birds; they could be one of the most important foods for humans. With 30 percent available oil by weight, hemp oil is the best known source of essential omega-3 and other essential fatty acids, and is touted as a powerful immune-system builder. Not only are hemp seeds good for us, but they taste good too. If they were available, they would most certainly be welcome on bagels, next to the illicit poppy seed bagel. In the Netherlands and in Germany, hemp breakfast cereal is commercially successful and is enjoyed by law-abiding middle-class weight watchers.

Rubbing hemp seed oil on your body is recommended as well. Any good drug store or head shop should be able to provide you with an assortment of balms, soaps, cosmetics and topical creams whose base is hemp seed oil. The cost of these products is still higher than their petrochemical and corn-based counterparts, but hemp enthusiasts assure us that the prices would fall radically were the industry unfettered by prohibition and prejudice.

> We recommend that the American Farm Bureau Federation encourage research into the viability and economic potential of industrial hemp production in the United States. We further recommend that such research include planting test plots in the United States using modern agricultural techniques.
>
> —*American Farm Bureau Federation resolution*

You can burn hemp seed oil, too. Before Europeans discovered whaling, and, later, Standard Oil, hemp seed oil was a valued source of light, heat, and energy. Henry Ford didn't, as far as we know, rub hemp seed oil on his body, but he did build and fuel a car with it. In the early 1930's Ford had invested in the development of biomass conversion at an experimental farm at Iron Mountain, Michigan, where he produced plastics, lubricating and fuel oils, and tinkered with the idea of running his entire manufacturing enterprise on biomass fuel based on large-scale hemp farming. This was about the time they were prohibiting the hemp trade in Washington. Were it not for the Marijuana Tax Act and the international Single Treaty on Drugs, we may have been burning non-toxic, renewable hemp oil for the last 50 years, instead of fighting Desert Storms.

And there is no known limit to the number of things hemp fiber is said to be good for. The hemp stalk is a long, strong weed with a thick, spongy core. The tough fibers on the outside are what we make cloth and rope out of. In the fiber business, size counts. The longest fibers are the best. The average length of hemp fibers is about fifteen inches. The next best fiber source, flax, has an average length of about three inches, and is currently the main source of fine linen. Hemp fiber, when finely groomed and woven, is softer than silk and more resilient than cotton.

The by-product of hemp fabric–making includes all the white stuff in the middle of the reed, the cellulose, from which we get paper, and biomass fuel. There is a lot of this by-product. Enough to consider the production of methanol, which when combined with hemp seed oil could power a nation and turn world economies on their heads. Technologies that were introduced at about the same time as the grass prohibition allowed producers to separate the long fibers from the white, spongy stuff quite elegantly. At the time that this "hemp decordicator" was introduced to the United States, hemp production was at about the same level as cotton before Eli Whitney and his cotton gin brought cotton into the modern industrial era. The significance of any coincidence between the patenting of a practical hemp decordicator and the prohibition of its raw material is something that we can leave to investigative journalists and other suspicious minds.

In some parts of Europe, hemp farming is making a comeback, in other parts, it never went away. Eastern Europe has been a hotbed of hemp cultivation since the Scythians arrived a millennium ago. Although smoking grass is not unknown in places like Poland and Lithuania, most Europeans seem chiefly interested in the stems and seeds, from which they have always made cloth, oils, ropes and fuel.

The Dutch, for example, have long counted on hemp as a mainstay of their economy. Today's coffee shops and narco-tours make a significant economic impact, but they pale in comparison to the vast family fortunes amassed during the golden age of *hempf,* when Dutch traders ruled the seas under hempfen sails, and the country was quite literally tied together by hemp. In fact, the word *canvass* is Dutch for cannabis. Holland's population was made up of merchants and farmers. The merchants sent sailing ships around the globe under hempfen sheets, exporting the fruits of the land, and returning with bags of money and useful things to sell back to the farmers. Hemp was the fuel of the economy; it was hemp ropes that networked the canals, and hemp sails that took Dutch produce abroad.

Hemp is not only useful for humans, it's also good for Earth. It does not deplete the soil of nutrients, it does not require the use of pesticides or irrigation, when it burns it does not produce toxic gasses, and in the autumn it provides fibers that could make much of the pulp industry redundant. We wouldn't have to chop down virgin rain forests.

This is not very good news if you own a pulp mill or an oil well, or if you sell pesticides or planted a patch of *ruderalis canadianis* in the out-back, but if you own an Earth, growing hemp would seem to be in your best interests. Farmers, who do own an Earth, tell us that growing hemp reinvigorates damaged soil and pays bills; engineers tell us that *Cannabis sativa* will draw toxins out of waste sites and prepare deforested areas for new growth.

People who believe that there is money to be made and an Earth to be saved are not a cabal of pot-smoking tree huggers. They are business people, environmentalists, farmers, town councilors, high rise glaziers and lumbermen. They make knapsacks and bumper stickers, two by fours and pinafores, massage oil and diesel fuel, soap, beer, pastilles, blue jeans, and insul bricks.

They make web sites, have conventions, and try to distance themselves from the Rastafarians and the tree huggers. The hemp lobby looks more like an Amway army than a new-age conspiracy.

We know that hemp will grow in nearly every habitable corner of the globe, that it may be a practical alternative to fossil fuel addiction and deforestation of the rest of the planet, and that it has the side benefit of providing humans with the means of temporary escape from the drudgery of life. Some people appear to believe the latter is sufficient reason to prohibit the cultivation of hemp plants entirely.

The economy of hemp need not be an economy of prosecuting attorneys and urine testing. There is real money to be made in the growing, processing, manufacturing and distribution of *Cannabis sativa* and her cousins. Consider now that the chief impediment to using all this great stuff is that it makes people feel good for a couple of hours, then makes them fall asleep.

Chapter 7
A Pharmacological Cornucopia

GANJA IS MORE THAN JUST A PLANT SMOKED FOR FUN BY CURIOUS KIDS AND bohemian businessmen — and more, indeed, than a cleaner replacement for crude oil or cotton or pulp. If the medical library is anything to go by, then cannabis is a veritable treasure trove of useful pharmaceuticals. There are health benefits to be had from almost every part of the plant, both immediately and by extension. From root to seed the cannabis plant provides us with everything from topical antibiotics to essential fatty acids, while the consequences for human health of a pesticide-free, agriculturally based industrial economy are beyond measure. It is tempting to venture into an exploration of the many medical applications of *Cannabis sativa,* but an afternoon at the public library or a few hours on the Internet will give the interested reader ample information concerning its many medical applications. This, however is chiefly a book about the euphoric effects of cannabis, and so we shall restrict ourselves to a look at the psychotropic applications. This means we are looking at the resinous flowers that people like to smoke.

People who smoke grass do so because it makes them feel good. Ask anyone you know who smokes marijuana. It makes them feel good. But what does this mean? What, exactly, does smoking cannabis flowers do? For an expert description of the "high," we turn to the Addiction Research Foundation in Toronto, Canada.

The High Defined

At low to moderate doses, 5mg of THC or less, the user may experience ... disinhibition, garrulousness, relaxation, drowsiness, feeling of well-being, euphoria, distortions of the perception of time, body image and distance, increased auditory and visual acuity, enhanced tactile, olfactory, kinesthetic and gustatory senses, spontaneous laughter, impairment of recent memory, mild confusion, decreased concentration, decreased muscle strength and balance, impaired ability to perform complex motor tasks, fearfulness, anxiety and panic or even mild paranoia.

At high doses, 10-30 mg THC or more, intensification of the low-dose effects may occur as well as any of the following: synesthesias, pseudo-hallucinations, impaired judgment, slowed reaction time, confusion, impaired performance of simple motor tasks, depersonalization, pronounced paranoia, agitation, extreme panic, and even true hallucinations.[10]

So in other words, what happens when someone smokes a joint?

A mild euphoria envelopes the smoker, causing her immediate concerns to recede temporarily, and replaces them with any number of a myriad of effects noted above. At a modest dose, depending on the particular blend of psychoactive cannabinoids, she might expect to feel giddy and jittery at first, maybe confused and paranoid for a short time and later, she will become somber, relaxed, talkative, hungry, maybe sexy, and finally, sleepy. Her senses will not report a "normal" state of reality; time will seem slower or faster than normal; smells, tastes, even vision and touch may become more acute.

Her environment, frame of mind, and intended purpose will have a great effect on determining the "high" she will experience. In general, smoking a marijuana cigarette produces a mild sense of disorientation and sometimes panic, followed by a couple of hours of gentle euphoria, a tendency toward self examination, hunger, and gradual sleepiness. This is why people like to smoke it: It makes them feel good.

The Forbidden Medicine

To simply say that smoking grass makes some sick people feel better would be an irresponsible oversimplification, but essentially, it is true. Many patients turn to marijuana for comfort, pain relief, ease from their symptoms, and distraction. They and their doctors have determined that cannabis is useful.

> Long-term or terminal illness takes its toll on the spirit, and can give rise to mood disorders that can destroy a viable patient. People who are sick, or in chronic pain, or are under a viral death sentence, often suffer depression. Doctors prescribe a broad spectrum of therapies to help ease the tired, worrisome minds of their sickly patients. Currently, such patients are offered counseling and medications like Prozac and Valium. This may be all well and good, but a growing number of doctors and patients are asking to use cannabis flowers as a part of their treatment.
>
> In short, sometimes old age seems to present a daunting parade of gloomy displeasures and discomforts. And when all these natural burdens accumulate, help is hard to get. Well, it may be easy to get Prozac or lithium. Hard to get is what may be the best medicine — marihuana.[11]

The long tradition of using resinous cannabis flowers in the treatment of disease is supported by a mountain of modern, scientific study into its health risks and benefits. There is so much information about cannabis and its effect on the human body and mind that one can only measure it by the pound. To evaluate it all would be a life's work. Doctor Lester Grinspoon,

author of *Marihuana: The Forbidden Medicine,* is a professor of medicine at
Harvard University who has made the study and evaluation of the cannabis
literature his life's work. He concludes that it is a remarkably safe and useful
pharmacological cornucopia.

> What these reviews and others show is, first, that marihuana is
> remarkably safe. In 5,000 years of medical and nonmedical use, it has
> never been known to cause a single overdose death.... Marihuana has
> fewer serious side effects than most prescription drugs and is far less
> addictive or subject to abuse than many drugs now used as muscle
> relaxants, sedatives, and painkillers. ...
>
> As more and more patients approach them [physicians] with questions
> about marihuana, they will have to provide answers and make recom-
> mendations ... They will have to learn which symptoms and disorders may
> be treated better with marihuana than with conventional medications.
>
> Even today, the greatest danger of using marihuana medically is not
> impurities in the smoke but illegality, which imposes much unneces-
> sary anxiety and expense on suffering people.[12]

Another source we should be able trust is the United States Drug
Enforcement Agency. Francis J. Young, U.S. D.E.A. Chief Jurist, decided
after years of hearings and study that grass was "one of the safest therapeuti-
cally active substances known to man."[13]

Alphabet Soup

Cannabis flowers are used to induce euphoria. They almost certainly have
some other properties, but the use of the psychoactive flowertops is pretty
much restricted to the production of a state of euphoria in the patient. The
use of euphoric hemp in the treatment of mental, spiritual, and physical ail-

ments has a very long history. In ancient China these flowers were wafted around the sickroom, presumably as an analog for their oral application.

There are a number of conditions that appear to benefit from altering the consciousness of a patient. Bipolar disorders, epilepsy, depression due to illness, geriatric depression, or chronic pain are among them, as are some of the effects of chemotherapy, HIV infection and glaucoma. Most of these conditions and the related treatments are in the area of mental or spiritual health and are directly related to the euphoric effects of cannabis.

> Euphoria: A word used to express well-being, or the perfect ease and comfort of healthy persons, especially when the sensation occurs in a sick person.
>
> —*Oxford Complete Dictionary of the English Language*

Some authorities insist that cannabis flowers must be replaced by modern pharmaceuticals; synthetics are safer, more effective, and more easily controlled. This may even be true, but a growing number of physicians and patients find that the synthetic replacements are not as effective as the natural herb. Most medical users of grass would be happy to use a synthetic substitute if they could get one that worked like cannabis flowers.

Resin glands of cannabis plants contain a variety of psychoactive chemicals, the most obvious of which is THC. THC is one of many psychoactive substances that have been identified in the cannabis flower. Some authorities insist that THC is the only active substance in cannabis — apparently in the face of all the evidence — and have licensed synthetic THC products for pharmaceutical use. The synthetic substitutes (like Drobinol) contain only THC, since the authorities insist that THC is the only active chemical in cannabis.

Some cannabis flowers will make a person jumpy, while others will make them sluggish. This is common knowledge. What modern science has discovered, however, is that the different "high" is related to the various proportions of THC and other cannabinoids, of which there seem to be an endless list. The roll call includes olivetol, cannaflavon, cannabigerol, cannabidiol, and cannabinol, all of which have an active part to play in altering the consciousness of the user.

Cannabis connoisseurs have known this for a long time. They never knew the names of the chemicals, but they knew the different "high" produced from a willowy high-country hashish or a lush lowland smoke. Nepalese hashish, for example, is not just stronger than other smokes, it is chemically different from its cousins. Anybody who has ever smoked it knows this intuitively. This author has never met a Nepalese hashish connoisseur who was agnostic.

One Size Fits All

THC is not marijuana. It is a powerful psychoactive substance that can be used to benefit some sick people. Taking a THC capsule it is not like smoking marijuana. Pure THC capsules do not have the buffering effects of other cannabinoids, and they cannot be moderated by the patient. If a patient takes a toke or two of real grass, and decides that they have had enough, they stub out the joint, and go about their business. With the synthetic substitutes they are subject to all the familiar variables of cannabis stimulation, but they have no control over dosage. They may be in pain or panic, but they have no control over the wave of THC. One size fits all.

Sufferers of serious illness are provided with a chemical analog of cannabis flowers, which doesn't work like cannabis flowers, and are told that it is the best that science and law can offer. Sick people can have Drobinol, barbiturates, electroshock therapy; they can have Demerol, morphine, or lobotomy, but they cannot have cannabis flowers, because our lawmakers have determined that cannabis flowers are too dangerous even to be prescribed under the supervision of a doctor.

Even William F. Buckley Knows This

Even the right-wing American demagogue William F. Buckley, Jr., knows that this is wrong. His column in the *National Review* never fails to amuse and instruct. In 1995, he told us that an ailing family member asked him to get her some pot while undergoing chemotherapy. Buckley found himself faced with the prospect of ruin, under a streetlight on the wrong side of Washington, D.C., on the one hand, and the needless pain of his little sister on the other. The lesson was not lost on that self-described "right-wing encephalophone," who confessed, out loud, both his cowardice and his outrage at the American prohibition of cannabis medicine:

> But ... big brother is a coward, and there is just that chance that a lurking narc would spot him paying cash for enough marijuana to relieve baby sister and decide that was a dreamy photo op ...[14]

When Munchies Become Essential

Aside from producing a state of euphoria and inducing introspection, cannabis flowers provide another tremendous benefit to sick people. Pot smokers refer to the effect as "the munchies"; a physician might refer to it as a miracle. This is no joke. People who are enduring chemotherapy, depression, and chronic pain often suffer from wasting syndrome, the inability to take sustenance. Cannabis flowers may not be the only therapy that can produce a desire to take food, but it is reported to be among the best. Grass does not just make a user hungry, it also provides an antiemetic that helps keep the food down.

There is broad support for the prescription of cannabis flowers in the treatment of a spectrum of diseases. Medical authorities would like to use cannabis, or an analog, in their practice, but in many jurisdictions it is absolutely forbidden. A doctor will lose her privilege to write prescriptions for associating herself with this medicine. There is such a stigma attached to the use of grass that people will go to any lengths to provide the medical benefits of it without allowing the patient to feel the "high."

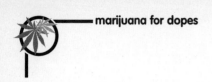

Pigheaded Science

A team of researchers in Israel may have come up with a solution. They call it Anandamide, after the Sanskrit *ananda* — eternal bliss. William Devane and Raphael Mechoulam of Hebrew University have spent nearly 30 years researching cannabis and its effects on the brain. Mechoulam was the discoverer of delta-9-THC, and more recently has made inroads into the development of a "high-free" synthetic.

The human brain has a limited number of natural receptors to which a foreign substance can "bind." Surprisingly, some of these receptors are for compounds only found in cannabis. It would seem that the human body is prepared for, or has evolved a receptivity for, ganja. A *Science* magazine article outlined Mechoulam and Devane's extraction of an oily "grass-like" substance carefully produced from the mashed brains of pigs. This extract, Anandamide, will mimic THC and occupy the brain's natural grass receptors without providing the characteristic euphoria.

Anandamide may hold the key to providing sufferers of epilepsy, Tourettes Syndrome, cerebral palsy, and other disorders with symptomatic relief without making the patient "high." Many hundreds of thousands of dollars have gone to fund this important research, while the relatively cheap, natural, and effective substance could be made readily available through a few strokes of the legislator's pen. It is difficult to avoid the conclusion that the reason cannabis flowers are legally withheld from sick people is that it might not only relieve symptoms, but it may also make them feel good.

> You shut your eyes in frustration. If somebody discovered that marijuana would cure AIDS, would the narcs still prowl the streets?
>
> — *William F. Buckley*[15]

Chapter 8
Cannabis in Religion

IN MUCH OF THE MODERN SCIENTIFIC LITERATURE REGARDING THE EFFECTS of cannabis, researchers report a "depersonalization" effect. In most studies, this effect is noted, but not elaborated upon. In an examination of the religious and spiritual uses of cannabis, this depersonalization is central.

> Depersonalization. A state in which a person's sense of the "reality" or existence of his mind or body is weakened or lost.
> —*Le Dain Commission Report on Cannabis, p. 392*

"Depersonalization" is the whole point of smoking cannabis. People smoke it in order to alter their "sense of reality" and their sense of self. Musicians smoke it to alter their sense of reality out loud. Poets smoke it to clear away their left-brain function and wax unencumbered. Lawyers use it to forget about lawyering for a few hours. Seekers use it to find their way.

We know that the use of cannabis for euphoric purposes is an ancient practice among humans. When people smoke grass, they lose their accustomed sense of time and space, their ability to connect events and ideas is altered. We call this depersonalized state "euphoria."

> Euphoria: a mood or emotional attitude of invulnerability or "all is well": the individual has an intense sense-feeling of health and vigor, often despite real somatic disabilities (which are ignored). In pathological cases, unsystematized and transient delusions to fit the mood are generated: the person has a million dollars, the strength of an ox, or is ruler of the universe.[16]

Whether cannabis euphoria provides delusion or access to another reality is a question we may not be able to answer, but the belief in the latter has been with us for a very long time. Any good library can provide volume after volume on the subject of its religious and ritual employment. Cannabis has played a part in the history of most of the major western religions, and writers have left no turn unstoned in exploring the place of grass in scripture and in sacred rites. If everything that has been written about the nature and role of cannabis in various world religions can be believed, dope smoking should be considered a sacrament, not a crime.

Qunubu

Earlier in this book, we imagined Ts'ai Lun, the ancient Chinese paper maker rubbing cannabis to prepare the fibers, licking the sticky cannabinoids off of his fingers. Professor Richard E. Schultes, director of the Harvard University Botanical Museum, and the world's leading ethnobotanist posits a similar picture:

> Early man experimented with all plant materials that he could chew and could not have avoided discovering the properties of cannabis, for in his quest for seeds and oil, he certainly ate the sticky tops of the plant. Upon eating hemp, the euphoric, ecstatic and hallucinatory

aspects may have introduced man to an other-worldly plane from which emerged religious belief, perhaps even the concept of deity. The plant became accepted as a special gift of the gods, a sacred medium for communion with the spiritual world and as such it has remained in some cultures to the present.[17]

In the groves and temples of ancient Mesopotamia, people worshipped a diversity of gods and goddesses. We know that burning incense was a common practice at the time.[18] The worship of female deities seems to be particularly connected to the incense offering. Further evidence indicates that this incense burning was no idle sacrifice: worshipers inhaled the incense. They inhaled incense to get in touch with their gods.

So what was this incense? The planet is littered with psychoactive substances that could have provided an altered state. The most respected sources on the subject of botanical and religious history assure us that the incense was grass, probably hashish or hashish oils blended with other psychoactive and aromatic herbs.

> It is said that the Assyrians used hemp as incense in the seventh and eighth century before Christ and called it "Qunubu," a term apparently borrowed from an old East Iranian word "Konaba," the same as the Scythian name "cannabis."[19]

So the term *qunubu* was "apparently borrowed from an old East Iranian word," which suggests that the practice of burning incense, or at least knowledge of cannabis, is older than the Assyrian civilization, which takes us back into unrecorded history.

The Word Spread

Or is it unrecorded? The Hindu book of knowledge, the Vedas, predate any other remembered human or divine history. Reaching back beyond 6000

BCE, these books form the basis of religion for hundreds of millions of people. And the Vedas recommend the use of hemp as a sacrament. In the Rig-Veda, the Sanskrit word for cannabis is *canna,* and it is told how Siva brought it down from the mountains so that people could enjoy it as his blessing. The people of the Hindus Valley were said to be Aryan invaders from the west. Most likely from Persia. To this day, Siva and cannabis — bhang — are so intimately connected that millions of people give praise to Siva before drawing on a chillum or sipping a bhang lassie. It may only be coincidence, but even at the turn of the twenty-first century, the world's most potent hemp plants grow in the precise location from which Siva is said to have brought it: Hindu Kush.

The Vedas tell the story of how *canna* came into the hands of human beings, but how did the Sanskrit word *canna* get all the way from Northern India 8,000 years ago to the East Iranians and later Assyrians, who called it *Qunubu,* and the Europeans, who call it "cannabis"? It doesn't take a linguistic anthropologist to figure out that these cultures must have had more in common than is generally assumed.

The word *cannabis* comes to us from the Scythians. We can see that the root of this word comes to us from the Sanskrit Vedas (*canna*), but it raises the question of whether the Scythians' religious customs also echo those of the ancient Aryans from the Hindus Valley.

The Scythians are known among the Persians as "Sakas" and among the ancient Hebrews as the "Ashkenaz." They are believed to have originated in Persia, but they made the world their home. They were a fierce, wandering people whose influence was felt from the Russian Steppes to China. Many scholars give the Scythians credit for spreading cannabis and knowledge of its euphoric properties across Europe and much of the Middle East. The central place of hemp in their culture — for clothing, rope, and food — has survived them in the hemp-growing regions north of the Black Sea, and perhaps also in the occult religious customs of our forebears. The Greek historian Herodatus wrote, circa 450 BCE, about the Scythians' penchant for smoking pot, but until fairly recently, nobody believed him.

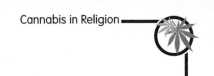

> They make a little tent, fixing three sticks in the ground, tied together and tightly covered with felt. Inside a dish is placed, with red-hot stones and some hemp seeds.
>
> The Scythians take kannabis seed, creep in under the felts, and throw it on the red-hot stones. It smolders and sends forth such billows of smoke that no Greek steambath could surpass it. The Scythians howl with pleasure at these baths, which serve them instead of bathing, for they never wash their bodies with water...[20]

Recent information has led scholars to believe that the Scythians did, in fact, bathe like everybody else. And they smoked a lot of dope. They were a matriarchal people who had both kings and queens, but the discovery of ancient tombs suggest that it was the queen who wore the pants in the cultural family. Among the remains found in their remarkable tomb sites are horses, servants, weapons, and hemp flowers. The Scythian nomads encountered by Herodatus may have had to make do with seeds and stems, but it seems that fine hemp linens and flower tops were considered an essential item for a queen on her way to the next life.

Ancient Hebrews

> Then God said, I give you every seed-bearing plant on the face of the whole earth, and every tree that has fruit in it.
>
> —*Genesis 1:29-30*

The authority of the Bible is called upon to fortify just about any theory or argument imaginable. People quote from it willy-nilly to back up theories as strange and unlikely as visitors from space, planetary collisions, and universal celibacy. When dopers quote the above passage from Genesis, they feel justified in twisting up a doobie, as if this passage gives them the green light to enjoy the forbidden herb. Their opponents can find any number of contradictory scriptural passages that argue for temperance, sobriety, and the avoidance of pleasures of the flesh.

But the Bible seems to be silent regarding the use or prohibition of cannabis specifically. Bible scholars do tell us of several references to something called *kaneh* or *kaneh-bosm*, which has been variously praised and prohibited in scripture. *Kaneh* and *kaneh-bosm* has been translated from the Hebrew as "calamus." The substance is some kind of aromatic herb that is mixed with spices and oil, and that is pleasing to God. Calamus is a common marsh weed that has no exotic properties and has never been regarded as a noble substance. Noah Webster tells us, in his 1940 edition, that:

> calamus [kaneh-bosm in scripture]: an aromatic substance obtained from some kind of reed or cane.

Modern scholars have presented a convincing argument that the Biblical *kaneh* was our weed. If the Biblical "calamus" or *kaneh-bosm* is actually cannabis, then the picture begins to look better for the Bible-toting pot smoker:

> Then the Lord said to Moses, "Take the following fine spices: 500 shekels of liquid Myrrh, half as much of fragrant cinnamon, 250 shekels of Kanna-bosm, 500 shekels of cassia — all according to the sanctuary shekel — and a hind of olive oil. Make these into a sacred anointing oil, a fragrant blend, the work of a perfumer. It will be the Sacred Anointing Oil.
>
> —*Exodus 30: 22-26*

The "Sacred Anointing Oil" was hash oil? Impossible. Perhaps. But consider the following: The ancient Hebrews traded with the Scythians and had intimate knowledge of their culture. The Scythians and their Persian brethren shared much of their history with the Hebrews, and it would be very unlikely that the Israelites were unaware of the "incense burning" among the tribes that surrounded them. Hashish was no idle recreation in the Middle East, it was at the heart of their religions and philosophies. It is difficult to believe that the Hebrews could have been unaware of, or uninfluenced by, the cannabis cults all around them.

> The reason for confusion and the relative obscurity of the role played by the Scythians in world history is explained by the fact that they were known to the Greeks as Scythians but to the Semites as Ashkenazi.[21]

If the Scythians and the Ashkenaz are one and the same people, then it is impossible to imagine that the Biblical chroniclers were unaware of the euphoric and religious applications of cannabis. It seems plausible, even likely, that the *kaneh* of the Old Testament was the Persian *canna*, the Scythian *cannabis*, and the Vedic *canna*, and that it was used in some ceremonies by some ancient Hebrews.

> You have not brought any kaneh for Me, or lavished on Me the fat of your sacrifices. But you have burdened Me with your sins and wearied Me with your offenses.
>
> —*Isaiah 43:23–24*

So how do things stand for the smoker looking for scriptural advice? The jury is definitely out. Those looking for reason to banish cannabis from religious worship can point to any number of passages condemning the practice of burning incense, while others might take the advice of Solomon, whose wisdom is said to be remembered by the hemp sewn over his grave.

So maybe some ancient Semites used cannabis incense in biblical days. But Deuteronomy tells us all about how those who burned incense to the goddess were rounded up and exterminated.

And He brought down the idolatrous priests, whom the king of Judah had ordained to burn incense in the high places in the cities of Judah, and in the places round about Jerusalem; Them also that burned incense unto Baal, to the Sun, and to the Moon, and to the Planets, and to all the Host of Heaven.

—2 Kings 23

Jesus Smoked Dope?

This seems to be Yahweh's final word on the subject. So we were through with all that incense burning by the time Jesus makes his appearance in Scripture. Maybe. But on the other hand, we find the Ethiopian Zion Coptic Church, whose scholars argue that they are the oldest Christian sect, and have remained outside the parry and thrust of official Christian dogmatic arguments since the time of Mark, around 50 CE. Their scripture includes the Gnostic passages of the Bible that were left out of later versions. They will tell you that the official Christian dogmatists have argued themselves out of the true sacrament that Jesus brought to mankind: cannabis. And they are serious. While it is probable that the historical Jesus was intimately familiar with the rites and ceremonies of incense-burning sects, it does not therefore follow that Jesus smoked dope.

Rasta Roots

For the Ras Tafari, ganja is the holy herb — the sacrament brought to man by Jesus as a blessing to the Israelites to instruct and comfort His people who were in exile in Babylon. The Israelites in this case are Africans, and Babylon is Jamaica.

The religion is rooted in the teachings of Marcus Garvey, a Jamaican rebel who in the 1920's and '30's pointed the way out of Babylon. With the coming of the Lion of Judah, Haile Selassie of Ethiopia, the people of Ras

Tafari would return to Africa and freedom. Their teachings are not exactly embraced by mainstream Christian churches. Wherever they have brought their message of freedom and ganja, they have been harassed, jailed, or deported. And it doesn't take a prophet to understand why: They have no churches, no scriptures, no leaders, no Swiss bank accounts, and although they use the language of Christianity, they provide only half-hearted scriptural arguments for their unique interpretation of the Bible.

They believe that God reveals himself to any pious seeker who smokes the herb and asks for instruction. Ras Tafari is not about Marcus Garvey or cock-eyed scriptures; Ras Tafari is a religion based upon each man's intimate and ongoing dialog with God. Smoking the holy herb is believed to provide a bridge between heaven and earth, and an insight into the mind of God.

Shaman You

Rastafarianism seems to have more in common with shamanism than it does with modern Christianity.

Virtually all shamanistic religions employ euphoric or hallucinogenic substances in their rituals. Modern witchcraft evolved out of the Magick of the alchemists of Persia, Lebanon, and Egypt who were convinced of the value of hashish in worship. Although much is yet to be learned about the uses of hemp drugs in the magical rituals of Wiccan ceremony, there is enough to suggest that cannabis has played a role.

> Drugs crop up chiefly in connection with witchcraft. Professor Michael Harner has recently argued that they were of central importance to witchcraft in Europe, but that this has been obscured by the fact that so much of the source material, most of it in Latin, has never been studied by anybody with an interest in this aspect of the subject. [22]

In Europe of the Middle Ages, magic was employed as a means of foretelling the future, and of influencing that future. And it was not only the wise women and soothsayers who regarded cannabis as an important part of their lives. The people of Europe relied on hemp to provide themselves with clothing, shelter, tools, and food. A farmer would hitch up his trousers as high as possible when sewing his hemp seeds in order that he might cause the plant to grow taller. Young girls would throw hemp seeds over their shoulders to predict their fortunes.

> In the Balkans, an ancient folk ritual (still practiced in the early part of the twentieth century) involved not so much dancing, as running through a circle of burning hemp. As the peasants scampered through the flames, they chanted.[23]

Cannabis has been known to occultists and practitioners of Magick for centuries. Aleister Crowley, the late renaissance aspirant, understood the properties of hashish and recommended its use. Crowley was an adept in a broad spectrum of occult arts and believed cannabis to be the Tree of Knowledge of Genesis fame. He did not consider this tree evil or forbidden, since he believed that knowledge is, in principle, always to be preferred to ignorance: "Nay! For I am of the serpent's party; Knowledge is good, be the price what it may."[24] After searching his soul under the influence of visionary doses of hashish, Crowley concluded that he approved. Very definitely: "This ceremonial intoxication constitutes the supreme ritual of all religions."[25]

From all this ancient history, we might be led to believe that the use of cannabis as a religious object has fallen out of vogue, that religion has evolved beyond the need for euphorics. Incense, after all, is just incense.

Tell that to the followers of the Universal Church of God, or those brethren and sisteren at the Followers of Jesus, or the Rastafarians. A quick scamper across the Internet will turn up modern marijuana cults dedicated to Baal, Ashera, Jesus, Bast, Ja, and various other deities. And most shamanistic cults don't exactly have access to, or interest in, web sites. The Council on Spiritual Practices hosts a web site "dedicated to making direct experience of the sacred more accessible to more people." Those interested in the minutia of the sacred psychedelic experience should go and visit them.

Deuteronomy

Historically, psychoactive plants have played a major and likely formative role in many of the world's religions. Currently, the Native American Church and other spiritual groups around the world incorporate entheogens in their practices. Their experience suggests that the careful use of entheogens can bring rich returns with minimal risks.[26]

If there is a conclusion to be drawn from all of this, it is surely that the process of depersonalization or "getting high" has been and continues to be important in many religious rituals. It has often been a controversial practice, sometimes held secret from the many by the ecclesialastical few, sometimes scorned by the few and enjoyed by the many.

While the practice of eating herbs or inhaling incense as a sacrament may be repugnant to many people, we should really step back and decide whether or not it is a practice we, as a society, wish to prohibit, or wish to tolerate.

Chapter 9
Cannabis Culture in the 21st Century

AS WE ENTER THE TWENTY-FIRST CENTURY, CANNABIS CULTURE IS AS POTENT as it ever was in Dutch mercantile society or in Babylonian temples. Daily newspapers around the globe bring us the news about cannabis. Olympic medallists fail urine tests for marijuana metabolites; *New Scientist* magazine accuses the World Health Organization of suppressing reports on their embarrassing marijuana studies; the process of European unification is stifled over the issue of cannabis laws in the Netherlands and Germany; basketball All Star millionaires are dragged through the courts on charges of smoking doobies in the locker room after a game; editorials bristle with arguments for and against prohibition; Internet searches for marijuana sites return 25 million pages with information about grass. The world has become a virtual dagga cult!

Cannabis culture continues to enjoy a significant role in the business of being human. The most obvious role is that of agent provocateur. In centuries past, grass was important for agriculture, transportation, trade, medicine, and religion. The fact that our current interest in grass is chiefly on account of its legal status may be unfortunate, but it nonetheless affirms the enduring association between cannabis and human beings.

Amid the media noise in Washington, D.C., in 1998 about whether or not the President of the United States had a dangerous liaison with a White House intern, an interesting story had been shuffled to the back pages. It seems that in the urinalysis of bureaucrats and spin doctors, a considerable amount of evidence of cannabis consumption had given some high-profile narcs and staffers cause for embarrassment.

The controversy arose when Secret Service agents told Congress that at least 21 Clinton White House staffers had been toking, snorting, and tripping on LSD within a year prior to being granted security clearances. Exactly how the Secret Service knows this is, well, secret; but the President intervened on behalf of his staff and saved their smoked bacon. We assume that they, like the President, did not inhale. The fact is, a considerable number of the denizens of the halls of power are former pot smokers. The Clinton list, headed by the President himself, allegedly includes Vice President Al Gore, Interior Secretary Bruce Babbitt, Health and Human Services Secretary Donna Shalala. Former Republican House Speaker Newt Gingrich is also a suspect. And of course, George W. Bush, the new president for the new century, enjoys a reputation close to that of John Belushi's Animal House creation, Bluto. In between the (very) numerous tales of W's drinking excesses and the continual wispers of his decade-long infatuation with good Colombian blow, don't you think the odd spliff made a much welcome stop in the frat boy's hands? Likely indeed.

Nobody has noticed any amotivational syndrome among these high achievers (Boy George possibly excepted). Neither have they found evidence of any more than the normal pattern of brain atrophy in the bureaucracies. Unless you count the alleged sexual dalliances of the ex-president himself, but as we know, he tried marijuana but did not inhale, so we can't blame the pot for his apparent lack of sexual judgement. They do seem, however, to give credence to the "gateway" theory; they have moved up from craving pot to craving power.

And it's not just in Washington that important government positions are occupied by victims of the evil weed. In London, the remains of a reefer were recently found in an ashtray in the smoking room at the Treasury departmental offices, not 30 seconds' walk from the headquarters of the United Kingdom's chief narc, Keith Hellawell. We trust that the offending doper in the Treasury was not arresting crooks or counting money that day.

In the 1960's, the *Times* of London ran the infamous SOMA advertisement calling for the government to address the issue of cannabis in British society. The result of this lobby activity was the Wootten Report, which was summarily ignored, and is discussed earlier in this volume.

> The law against marijuana is immoral in principle and unworkable in practice...[27]
>
> —*The Times, July 27, 1967*

In the final months of 1997, another of the U.K's leading newspapers, *The Independent,* called for the nation to once again address the issue of prohibition. This time, they were not asking the government to study grass, since this has been done ad nauseum, but were plainly asking the government to respect the will of the majority and to stop fining and jailing citizens for smoking it.

The Independent has printed editorials that not only call for decriminalization, they have backed this up with testimonials from leading lawyers, doctors, cops, and cooks. Once again they are lining up the Who's Who of British society to give testimony before the open court of the daily press. Richard Branson, Jon Snow, and Anita Roddick, OBE, are among those calling on the government to bring the laws into accord with the times.

> I support decriminalization. People are smoking pot anyway and to make them into criminals is wrong. It's when you're in jail that you really become a criminal. That's where you learn all the tricks.[28]
>
> —*Sir Paul McCartney*

Other governments are being faced with similar demands. Canada offers an example of the legal gymnastics politicians and law enforcement agencies will resort to in dealing with the grass issue. In 1923, the Canadian government decided, for reasons that are far from clear some 75 years later, to include *Cannabis indica* in its new list of prohibited substances. The government of the day was led to believe that grass was an evil weed that caused immediate insanity and violent bloodbaths among its unwashed addicts. Since Canadians don't like bloodbaths or uncontrollable insanity, or especially unwashed addicts, they acted immediately and decisively. From that day to this, possession of cannabis in Canada has been an offense of varying degrees of gravity, depending on the political climate.

Every once in a while, the Canadian government reviews all the literature about grass and recommends that they stop putting people in jail for smoking it. Then they think about those bloodbaths and insanity, and double or reduce the jail terms instead. A few years later, they will commission a new study and ignore its recommendations. It's become a habit in Canada.

Canada Bans This Book

Once in a while, a government does something really stupid, and they come off looking as though they were asleep at the switch. Such was the case with Section 462.2 of the Criminal Code of Canada. For the lawmakers and newshounds of the day, the 1988 amendment to the code consisted of a couple of paragraphs in a desk-load of legislation, and almost nobody seems to have examined it very closely. All but one Members of Parliament raised their hands as they blithely revoked the Charter freedoms enshrined in the Canadian constitution.

Section 462.2 made the sale or possession of such things as waterpipes, grow lights, and the book you are reading a criminal offense. Section 462.2 strictly prohibited anything that advocates or assists in the use or traffic in cannabis and a broad list of other contraband substances. It allowed no appeal or exception on journalistic, educational, scientific, scholarly, or political grounds.

The Canadian people were sleeping as soundly as their legislators. There were no parades in the Peace Gardens, no Canadian Library Association freedom of information campaigns. Some important Canadian libraries even "weeded" their collections of *High Times* magazines and similar titles, not wishing to expose themselves to criminal charges and lawyer's fees. Head shops dropped like ducks in season, and most Canadians were only dimly aware that a law had been passed that contravened any civilized notion of freedom of speech.

The Canadian government had unwittingly succeeded in outlawing not only cannabis itself, but the activities and symbols of its attendant culture. A tee shirt with a marijuana leaf on it could get you a hundred thousand dollar fine and six months in the slammer. A bong could get you the same. And the law seemed to be working. For four years, Canada slept while books and magazines were confiscated at the border, legitimate businesses were closed, and library shelves were scrutinized by coppers and self-regulating librarians. This is the sort of control that drug czars in Washington only dream about.

But the Canadian cops were asleep at the switch, too. They had this cool new law that enabled them to charge pretty much anybody they wanted to with an offense of some sort or other. Cannabis shirts, tattoos, blunt papers, bongs, magazines, books, Ph.D. theses — it was all illegal. Nobody complained much, because it was mostly kids or poor people who got busted. But one day, some cop in the suburbs of Toronto messed with the wrong guy. He arrested Umberto Iorfida.

Umberto Iorfida believes in cannabis. He likes it. A lot. He says so publicly. He gives out NORML pamphlets. He's the president of NORML, for heaven's sake. The NORML pamphlets tell people about the benefits of smoking grass, which, according to the Criminal Code section 462.2, was illegal. So, one day while he was giving away pamphlets advocating law reform, the police arrested him under the auspices of the aforementioned statute. Which was the worst thing they could have done. Charging a zealot with an offense that clearly interferes with his rights under any respectable charter of freedoms is not a good idea. History is rife with such blunders. We call these people heroes or martyrs.

Cannabis advocates came out of the closet to support Iorfida. Though the police dropped all the charges, Iorfida and company converted the coppers' bad pass into a blue-line interception. Iorfida, in turn, charged the police with obstructing his Charter rights. In a Newmarket court, Section 462.2 and its attendant regulations were dismissed as repugnant to society and in contravention of the Canadian constitution. This lower-court ruling has very little force in law, however, and in many parts of Canada you could be arrested for possession of the book you are holding. But it was a big win. Everybody knows that the law is unconstitutional so everybody ignores it.

It's always marvelous to see what a big win will do for a team of zealots. This soap-box issue gave birth to a vibrant sub-culture of growers, lawyers, publishers, head shops, hackers, hemp advocates, and tree huggers, which was not really the original intent of the amendment to the criminal code of Canada by the Member from Mississauga North.

In Canada today one can go to a newsstand and pick up a magazine about grass. In fact during the period of research for this book, it was difficult to find a Canadian magazine without the word "marijuana" in the table of contents. Most of these magazines would be in contravention of Section 462.2 of the Criminal Code, since most of them advocated a change in the laws. Today you can buy bongs on Yonge street, hemp shirts in Halifax, and "canna-beer" in Vancouver. And you can thank Umberto Iorfida. Ain't democracy great?

Canada is tired of the drug war. Polls indicate overwhelming support for cannabis law reform, farmers have demanded and won the right to grow hemp, doctors and patients are defiant in their insistence on using cannabis medicine, and the zealots are currently battering away at the front gates with Supreme Court challenges. Meanwhile, the courts are jammed with suburban teenagers whose crime was smokin' boo with their brothahs. In Vancouver, the police have raised a white flag in the war on pot, declaring that they would not accost anyone for smoking a little grass. They even ignored Vancouver's infamous Cannabis Cafe — a true Amsterdam-style cafe — for as long as they could stand it, and even then they did not lay any charges.

Cannabis culture is healthy in Canada today. Most Canadians don't care very much about it one way or another, since they don't smoke it, but hardly anybody thinks that people should be jailed or harassed for their choice of intoxicants. Canadians tolerate a broad spectrum of lifestyle choices and they pride themselves on this distinction from their brethren to the south. As the twenty-first century begins, the government that declared that it has no business in the bedrooms of the nation is feeling uncomfortable in the living rooms as well. The question on the lips of midnight tokers in the land of the midnight sun is, does the government have the courage to follow the example of the Netherlands?

Nederweed from Never Never Land

The Dutch are a civilized people. They take well-earned pride in their status as one of the most civilized and well-ordered cultures in history. Criminal activity is not tolerated by their governments, their courts, or their modern and efficient police forces. If you're gonna do something bad, don't do it in the Netherlands.

But in the Netherlands, if you want to smoke dope, you go to the local café, pick up a twist of Moroccan hashish or a bag of "Nederweed," and take it home for your private enjoyment. If you prefer, you can sit down and have a few puffs and a chat with your friends. You can even phone in your order and have it delivered like so much pizza. Nobody is going to throw you up against a wall or put your name in the paper if you have a bag of grass in your briefcase.

The Netherlands is a refined realm where people take their civic pride more sincerely than we are used to in North America. Dutch housekeepers scrub the sidewalks, and Dutch lawmakers believe that the punishment for an offense should not be more injurious to the citizenry than the offense itself. They take this sense of cleanliness and justice seriously. They are also pragmatic. The social cost of enforcing an unjust and unpopular law is often out of proportion to the benefits such a law will provide. This was the thinking behind the Dutch decriminalization of cannabis misdemeanors.

In consideration of the massive weight of evidence demonstrating the innocuous nature of marijuana smoking, and the unreasonably acute social costs associated with its prohibition, the Dutch took the high road: Distribution and use of "hard" drugs (narcotics) would be a serious criminal offense, while possession of "soft" drugs would be a non-criminal offense, governed and enforced or tolerated by local authorities.

Virtual decriminalization of marijuana was good for Holland. The money spent finding, prosecuting, and sometimes jailing pot-heads could be spent elsewhere in the community. But the reassignment of constables from cannabis patrol to productive work was not the only boon to the Dutch economy: Narcotourists from around the world fly into Amsterdam to fork over foreign currency for hotel rooms, restaurants, museum tours, and Nepalese temple balls. We are told that a connoisseur who knows his way around the hip crowd in Amsterdam can get royal Nepalese temple balls, for a price. Every one of these luxuries, including the royal Nepalese hashish or stick of majoon, is taxed by the government. After an evening at the theater, the bookstores, and a rice tafel dinner, narcotourists visit quiet cafes and smoke exotic hashish before floating quietly back to their hotels, leaving smiling taxi drivers and tax collectors counting their blessings.

In America, they say that the Dutch are "soft on drugs." The British call them "wet." In places like Prague, they call the Dutch "irresponsible." But it's not as though the Dutch government advocates the use of marijuana. In fact it is a controlled substance, and the laws governing its use are strict and complex. For instance, it is illegal to import the cannabis, like royal Nepalese temple balls, so a shopkeeper's inventory is not tax deductible, and the sale of these non-existent goods is subject to tax, thereby ensuring that if a retailer is going to make any money on the deal, the end product is an expensive luxury.

The Dutch laws governing "victimless crimes" are pragmatic and sociologically sound. A prohibition on marijuana was neither warranted, nor enforceable, so the Dutch government created appropriate laws to govern and protect society from the consequences. With the decriminalization of such victimless crimes as smoking cannabis, the Dutch relieved themselves of the burden of maintaining an unenforceable law and profited society at one and the same time.

Teach Your Children Well

Dutch parents, like parents everywhere, worry about their teenagers using drugs, but for the Dutch, the worry is more about the effects of the drugs, and not the personal safety of the teenager. In the Potsdam, your daughter and her collegiate friends might go out to a coffee house to smoke pot and drink fruit juice. She will undoubtedly meet some unsavory characters — chess players, amateur philosophers, or even other suburban boppers out for a few laughs. She might smoke too much hash, or fall in love with a poet, or both. Dutch parents certainly have a lot to worry about. Compare this to your teenage daughter driving into downtown Albuquerque to score a bag from a street vendor who almost certainly also sells heroin, handguns, crack cocaine, and teenage girls. This scenario alone should cause any parent who is concerned about the drug problem to consider the wisdom in Dutch Courage.

In the Netherlands, like everywhere else, the marijuana business is big. But there, the government regulates and participates on the trading floor of the "grass exchange." In 1994, the net economic impact of cannabis trade on the Dutch economy was more than five billion dollars. Compare this to the estimated 70 billion spent elsewhere eradicating it.

Dutch growers and scientists have pioneered the botanical research and development of cannabis. Seed companies in the Netherlands distribute potent seeds to home growers world wide. The sale of "Nederweed" itself has produced a cottage industry like no other in the world. Enthusiastic young scientists have developed strains that are rivaled only by those grown in British Columbia and the Hindu Kush mountains themselves.

And then there is the revenue from tourists who are attracted by more than just the tulips, chocolate, and cheese. Unfortunately for these visitors, their homelands seldom render such a sane response to cannabis possession.

If an overzealous visitor tries to smuggle a jar of "Red Dirt Ruderalis" home to France or the U.S.A, they may be thrown in jail for possession of a packet of euphoric herbs that the "drug smuggler" would have enjoyed in the privacy of his own home.

Outside of the Netherlands and a few municipal districts in neighboring countries, most of the world locks people up for the offense of smoking weed. Let's meet a few of these reprobates.

Perth County Green

Jake is a marijuana grower. He lives in Canada, in rural southwestern Ontario, where larger operations harvest tobacco, corn, fruit, and vegetables. Jake grows between 40 and 50 cannabis plants annually, and harvests between six and eight kilograms of flowertops. He does not sell his weed, because he considers that immoral. He grows this all for his own use. He will happily give some to a neighbor who asks for some, but he would no more charge money for marijuana than he would ask a dinner guest to pay for a glass of wine or a cob of corn.

Jake has a day job in town, and in the evenings, after coaching the local junior hockey team, he likes to sit and smoke a little pot with his teenage sons. Jake has been raided by provincial and federal drug squads, local ne'er-do-well teenagers, and organized thieves. He has been jailed, ripped off, and threatened by neighbors, but his biggest fear is not from the cops and robbers, but rather from the emerging industrial hemp lobby. In a neighboring county, local farmers have received permits to grow low-THC varieties of *Cannabis sativa.*

"If these guys start growing that lousy weed in my neck of the woods, my female plants will all go to seed and I'll be smokin' rope!"

Dangerous Lies

Paul is an undergraduate student at a mid-sized undergraduate college. He has been smoking grass since he was 14 or 15, and today makes regular use of it while relaxing with his house-mates.

"Yeah, we all smoke it when we can get it, which is most of the time," he says. "We grew seven different patches of it last year and the cops got four of 'em. They've got helicopters everywhere! They left little calling cards stapled to the trees after they ripped out all the plants, just to let us know who ripped us off."

Paul explains that he doesn't use any other drugs, except beer, but that he has tried most of the available hard and soft drugs. Having been subjected to all of the anti-drug messages throughout his primary and secondary school, he discovered that he had been lied to.

"They told me that pot would damage my brain, my lungs, my reproductive system and make me a sloth. I tried it in about grade 10. When I discovered that they were lying to me about pot, I figured I had to find out about other drugs for myself. I tried coke, mescaline, ecstasy — all the junk you don't have to shoot. But I didn't get hooked on drugs. I'll use pot, coffee and alcohol, but now that I know about other stuff, I know enough to stay away from it. I'm not an 'A' student, but I'm not exactly a turnip, either: Next year I'll graduate with a degree in cross-cultural studies, and I'm thinking about going to law school."

Janine the Junker

Janine is a dope peddler. She distributes about two pounds of high-grade grass every week, and supplements her earnings as a waitress with the profits.

"I never sell in the restaurant. I don't sell to strangers. I don't have to, since all of the people I sell to have friends, and I trust them to give my number to responsible people. Most of my customers are pretty straight. Lawyers, salesmen, government workers, housewives, carpenters, musicians — I've even got one guy who is a judge!"

Janine has been selling grass for nearly 15 years, and she has never been bothered by the police. Every week, her supplier drops by with a small duffel bag full of fresh, seed-free flowers which she divides into about 100 small bags and stores in the refrigerator. By the time the next supply arrives in seven or eight days, she has distributed most of the grass. After her supplier is paid, Janine earns between seven hundred and one thousand dollars. "I put it in the bank along with the tips from the restaurant," she smiles. "It's my old age pension. Maybe I'll go back to Europe..."

Do They Give You Grass in Jail?

Elba, one of Janine's customers, suffers from epilepsy. She does not smoke cannabis, because it makes her cough. She bakes it in bread, which she eats every morning.

"I use a lot of pot — about an ounce of Janine's sinsemilla every week. My health plan won't cover it, but Janine gives it to me at cost, so it's not too bad. But still, my husband sometimes has to work overtime to cover the cost."

Elba's doctor does not recommend cannabis for her condition; her doctor might otherwise lose his right to practice medicine. Over the years Elba has been on and off more pills than she can remember names for, and she insists that the only thing that gives her relief is Janine's weekly bag of dope.

"I haven't had a serious seizure in the last two years, but I wonder what would happen if I got busted ... I don't think they give you grass in jail, do they?"

Elba need not worry. In jails around the world, cannabis has a way of finding itself behind bars. Anybody who has ever done time will tell you that you can get anything you want in jail, for a price.[29]

Dig It

Grass is here to stay. No drug wars are going to give us a cannabis-free society. It's impossible. Too many people like to smoke it. It is too valuable as a medicine, a commercial commodity, and an agent provocateur. Since time uncounted, humans have stood in circles after work and passed around a chillum, a pipe, a blunt, or a reefer. Intoxication is close to the bone and cannabis, like alcohol, has been an enduring euphoric device. No drug czars are going to stem this flow of criminal activity. Why any drug czar would want to remains an open question, but they will certainly try, and will just as certainly fail.

CODA: Curious Crimes in Canada

I had coffee with a grave digger one afternoon. We met at the local public library, where I was on the Internet researching cannabis use among White House staffers and he was looking for something good to read. As it turned out, I had recently published a novel which I recommended without hesitation, and he had a story for me, too.

Ian was on the dole, waiting for the thaw in April, so he could go back to work at the graveyard. He used to drive a cab, but he's too stiff for that now. The spade work keeps his joints greased, he says. When I told him I was writing this book on grass, he pulled on his graying beard and told me about the little stash that he grows between the rows of former monsignors of the parish. He confided that planting it among the deceased priests ensures that there will be no nosy widows inspecting his herb garden.

I Can Dig It

Ian took his coffee black. We took our paper cups across the park adjacent to the library, where dog walkers and joggers patrolled the pavement and coffee drinkers occupied the benches in the unseasonably warm February afternoon. We stood underneath the stark winter bows of an oak tree, and my companion produced a panetello and sparked it to life. I told him it was a bit early in the day for me, but he insisted that it would be good for my sciatica.

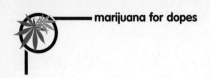

Everybody Must Get Stoned

At this very moment, the librarian who had signed me up for my half-hour session at the Internet terminal was crossing the park, heading in our direction. And we were smoking a joint in the early afternoon sunshine. Coffee in hand, pulling the shoulder up on her cardigan sweater, she was closing in on us, and I was ready to make a run for it. My companion, without missing a heartbeat, handed off the smoking reefer to the librarian, who glanced over her shoulder, took a long drag, and handed it back to the grave digger. A dog walker sniffed out our little circle and joined us for the last of the grave digger's joint.

It was an odd afternoon, I can promise you. I spent much of it at the beach, watching the waves roll in and thinking. Instead of writing. I was thinking about the dopers in the White House, and the grave digger in the park. I was thinking about cold nights under streetlights or stars where somebody lit a reefer and everybody stopped to think for an hour or so. Puppeteers and congressmen suddenly had something in common with ancient Semites and Scythian nomads. I thought about how long people had been doing this circle smoking thing, and why it seemed to be so important. Why is it so important that some people will put other people behind bars for smoking it, and others will risk these penalties to do so? I skipped some flat stones across the water and walked home.

I thought about our secret circle in the park, where a clutch of middle-aged strangers committed an offense worthy of incarceration. Right there in a Toronto park, under the noses of all and sundry. The butcher, the baker, and the candlestick maker, who made acquaintance in the park, committed an ancient act for which they were liable to imprisonment by a judge who gets his dope from a west-side short order waitress.

Notes

1. Officer W.F. Rowe in *The Consumer Union Report on Licit and Illicit Drugs.* Posted at <htttp://www.drugtext.org/reports/cu/CU59.html>.

2. *The Consumer Union Report on Licit and Illicit Drugs.* Posted at <htttp://www.drugtext.org/reports/cu/CU59.html>.

3. Quoted in Rowan Robinson, *The Great Book of Hemp,* p. 161.

4. Eva Bertram et al. *Drug War Politics,* p. 112.

5. For examples, see Michael Levine, *The Big White Lie*; Peter Dale Scott, *Cocaine Politics* and *The Iran-Contra Connection.*

6. Chris Conrad, Hemp: Lifeline to the Future, pp. 192-193, part of Chapter 16, "A World of Cannabis Cultures." Creative Xpressions Publications, Los Angeles, ISBN 0-9639754-1-2, http://www.pdxnorml.org/7_presidents.html

7. Roger Warner, *The Invisible Hand.*

8. Robinson, *The Great Book of Hemp.*

9. Chris Conrad, *Hemp: Lifeline to the Future,* p. 158.

10. T.C. Cox, M.R. Jacobs, A.E. LeBlanc, et al. *Cannabis in Drugs and Drug Abuse*, p. 212.

11. From Lester Grinspoon, *Excerpts from Marijuana*, pg. 12.

12. Lester Grinspoon and James Bakalar, "What the General Will Learn."

13. U.S. Department of Justice, Drug Enforcement Agency, "In the Matter of Marijuana Rescheduling Petition," [Docket #86-22] (1988, September 6), p. 57.

14. William F. Buckley, Jr. "Stupid law bars sick from smoking pot," p. 83.

15. Ibid.

16. Horace B. English and Ava Chapney English, *A Comprehensive Dictionary of Psychological and Psychoanalytical Terms*.

17. Richard E. Schultes, *Man and Marijuana*.

18. Geoffrey Parrinder, ed., *World Religions*.

19. Richard E. Schultes, and A. Hoffman. *Plants of the Gods*.

20. Herodatus, *The Histories*.

21. *Green Gold*, p. 80.

22. E. L. Abel, *The First 12,000 Years*, chap. 2, p. 7.

23. Brian Inglis, *The Forbidden Game*, p. 69.

24. Aleister Crowley, *The Psycholody of Hashish*, quoted in *Green Gold*, p. 252.

25. Ibid.

26. Council on Spiritual Practices.

27. SOMA advertisement, *The Times* (London), Monday, July 27, 1967.

28. *The Independent*, <www.independent.co.uk/sindypot/stories/cann06.htm>.

29. "Prison drug smuggling alleged," <http://www.pdxnorml.org/hn__34html>.

A Glossary for Dopes

Acapulco Gold — marijuana from the high country in Mexico, legendary for its pale green, almost golden color and its "heady" high.

Afghanistan — one of the major cannabis-producing regions. It's no longer safe to go there and buy fat slabs of their dense black hashish, but it is available in black markets across the world. Afghanistan is also home to a history of opium growing, so don't be surprised to find stripes of tan or white opium running through this hashish.

Anandamide — an extract made from mashed pig brains that mimics THC's effects on the brain without creating the euphoria associated with grass. Developed as a pharmaceutical alternative to medical marijuana. Proof that some people will go to any lengths to ensure that sick people will not get cannabis.

assassin — a killer; purportedly, the word is associated with the Arabic word for "hashish-eater" and the name given to a small Islamic sect formed in the 11th century CE that attacked European Crusaders heading to the Holy Land. According to the story, successful assassins were rewarded with **hashish**, which was said to give them a taste of the paradise which was their true reward.

bale — a compressed brick of marijuana, usually ranging in weight from 10 to 40 pounds.

bhang — a mildly intoxicating drink made from cannabis leaves. There are recipes for bhang lassies and other goodies all over the Internet.

blunt — a hollowed-out cigar filled with $^1/_8$ of cannabis and sealed with honey. No Bill Clinton jokes, okay?

bong — a water pipe. This is a very old method of smoking cannabis, found in almost every culture known to humankind.

boo — synonym for cannabis.

bud — synonym for cannabis.

buzz — a mild high.

Cannabis indica — botanical classification of cannabis first found in India.

Cannabis ruderalis — botanical classification of cannabis thought to have originated in Africa. Prior to the popular hobby of genetically engineering new strains, ruderalis was the rage among seed sellers; the strongest pot on the market. However, seed distribution web sites tell us that the markets are now calling for superstrains of indica and sativa — the products of ingenious "potanical" innovation.

Cannabis sativa — the botanical classification first given by Linnaeus in the 18th century. He chose "Cannabis" because that was the Scythian name for the plant (*cannabis*) and "sativa" (Xativa) for the Spanish town known for its fine hemp papers.

cannabutter — cooking ingredient made by simmering chopped cannabis leaves (**shake**) with butter.

charas — synonym for cannabis. In India, charas means hashish.

dagga — old southern African (Hottentot) synonym for cannabis.

delta-9-THC — argued to be "the active ingredient" in cannabis. In fact, there are a lot of "active ingredients," but THC takes the rap for a myriad of unpronounceable psychoactive substances.

doobie — marijuana cigarette, AKA joint, reefer, panatela, spliff.

dope — synonym for cannabis. Actually, dope is short for "dopamine," a naturally occurring analgesic substance produced in the human body.

Drobinol — synthetic **tetrahydrocannabinol** (THC). I have never heard of anyone taking this stuff (more than once) without medical supervision. AKA Marinol, synthetic THC.

gage — a synonym for cannabis. Probably related to the word "ganja." There are a lot of synonyms for cannabis.

ganja — one of the oldest synonyms for smokeable cannabis; argued to be derived from the same source as the river of the same name (Ganges). Today, the word ganja is most often associated with the Ras Tafari religion. Why? You would have to ask an botanical anthropologist.

grass — synonym for cannabis.

hash oil — like **hashish,** hash oil has a high concentration of THC and produces a very dense, potent smoke. The oil is usually painted on cigarette papers and rolled up with weed or tobacco. Hash oil varies in just about as many ways as its namesake, hashish. It can be very dark, gooey stuff that stinks to high heaven, or golden in color and as light and effective as penetrating oil.

hashish — cannabis resin cake; one of the most potent forms of psychoactives on the planet; can be smoked or eaten (*see* **Turkish Delight**). Color varies from black to dark brown to rusty red to green; may also be striped with opium.

hemp — just another synonym for cannabis; generally refers to stalks and stems of the plant used for the production of rope, textiles and paper. If anybody tells you that "hemp" is "marijuana's cousin" they are playing with the truth. "Hemp" usually refers to cannabis with very low THC content, and that allows people to grow it in places where its "cousin" is illegal.

herb — a respectful synonym for cannabis. Generally associated with Jamaican religious practice.

hit — a puff from a marijuana cigarette or pipe.

Jefferson Airplane — 1940s and '50s term for a roachclip improvised from a matchbook cover or a split match. If you heard their albums you would understand this.

jive –1930s and '40s slang for marijuana and marijuana-influenced popular music.

joint — a marijuana cigarette.

kif — golden hash or powdered cannabis flowers from Morocco.

Ma — a Chinese synonym for cannabis.

marijuana — the mother of all synonyms for cannabis; The story of how this modest little synonym became known world wide is a fascinating yarn, too long for a glossary, but too essential to the cannabis story to ignore completely . . .

majoon or **marjoon** — a traditional Moroccan confection made of powdered cannabis (kif or hashish), honey, fruit, nuts, spices, and the occasional bit of powdered lizard. Don't believe everything you read.

maryjane — another synonym for pot. *See* **marijuana**.

mezz — honest value; really great; the real stuff; in deference to Mezz Mezzrow, a good jazz musician and the greatest purveyor of jive in Harlem in the 20s and 30s.

muggles — 1930s and '40s slang for pot. This has nothing to do with Harry Potter or his mundane relations.

munchies — food cravings induced by smoking marijuana. This property of grass makes it helpful to sufferers of diseases that cause loss of appetite, such as AIDS.

Nepal — one of the major cannabis-producing regions. Home of the legendary Nepalese Temple Balls, the omega of hashish.

NORML — acronym for the National Organization to Reform Marijuana Laws, a North American group working to do just that. And getting there.

paraquat — an herbicide that some governments have sprayed on illegal marijuana crops. Some rabid lawmakers insist that the only good pot smoker is a dead pot smoker, and in the United States, Colombia and Mexico this deadly poison is used regularly to infect large marijuana plantations. Be careful who you vote for, and never inhale.

pot — Yep, another synonym for cannabis. Origin unknown.

reefer — American synonym for cannabis dating back to the early 1900s.

roach clip — an alligator clip or similar device used to hold **joints** that are too short to smoke without burning one's fingers. *See also* **Jefferson Airplane**.

roach — the roach is the last whiff of a joint, and some say, the most potent. You can find the origins of this term in Mexico, where they called it a *cucaracha*; and yes, that *is* what the song is about.

shake — cannabis leaves; the leafy part that aficionados don't smoke. Savvy growers use shake to make such things as hash/honey oil, cannabutter and bhang lassies.

sinsemilla — seedless cannabis; in myth, if not in truth, Jamaican growers tended the secret of sinsemilla for generations. Sinsemilla plants can be grown most easily from cloned cuttings from the "mother plant." Does this make the mother plant a virgin?

stoned — to be heavily under the influence of cannabis.

tea — a southern synonym for cannabis.

tetrahydrocannabinol (THC) — psychoactive agent found in high concentration in the resin glands of cannabis plants. *See* **delta-9-THC**.

toke — a puff of burning cannabis.

Turkish Delight — a sweet confection of palm syrup, dates, figs, almonds, cashews, and hashish.

weed — a naturally occurring synonym for cannabis

Sources

Abel, Ernest L. *Marijuana: The First 12,000 Years.* New York: Plenum Press, 1980.

Bennett, Chris, and Lynn Osborn. *Green Gold, the Tree of Life: Marijuana in Magic and Religion.* Frasier Park, CA: Access Unlimited, 1996.

Bertram, Eva, et al. *Drug War Politics: The Price of Denial.* Berkeley: University of California Press, 1996.

Brecher, Edward M., and the Editors of Consumer Reports Magazine. *The Consumer Union Report on Licit and Illicit Drugs.* N.p.: 1972. Posted at the International Foundation on Drug Policy and Human Rights web site. <http://www.drugtext.org/reports/cu/cumenu.htm>.

Buckley, William F., Jr. "Stupid Law Bars Sick from Smoking Pot," *National Review,* Feb. 6, 1995, p. 83.

Conrad, Chris. *Hemp: Lifeline to the Future.* Novalis, California: Creative Xpressions Publications, 1994.

———. *Hemp for Health: The Medicinal and Nutritional Uses of Cannabis Sativa.* Rochester, Vermont: Healing Arts Press, 1997.

Council on Spiritual Practices, <http://www.csp.org/pg.2>.

Cox, T.C., M.R. Jacobs, A.E. LeBlanc, et al. *Cannabis in Drugs and Drug Abuse.* Toronto: Addiction Research Foundation, 1983.

Crowley, A. *The Psycholody of Hashish,* quoted in Bennett and Osborn, *Green Gold,* p. 252.

"Da Smoke House 2001." Marijuana Glossary page at <http://dasmoke-house2001.cjb.net/>. Author unknown.

English, Horace B., and English, Ava Chapney, *A Comprehensive Dictionary of Psychological and Psychoanalytical Terms.* New York: Longmans, Green & Co., 1958.

Ginsberg, Allen. *Collected Poems, 1947–1980.* New York: HarperCollins, 1988.

Grinspoon. Excerpts from *Marijuana: The Forbidden Medicine* <http://www.rxmarihuana.com/excerpts.htm>.

Grinspoon, Lester, and James B. Bakalar, "What the General Will Learn," <http://www.rxmarihuana.com/playart.htm>.

Herodatus. *The Histories.* Berlin: Alfred A. Knopf Inc., 1997.

Inglis, Brian. *The Forbidden Game: A Social History of Drugs.* London: Hodder and Stoughton, 1975.

Levine, Michael. *The Big White Lie: The CIA and the Cocaine/Crack Epidemic.* New York: Thunder's Mouth Press, 1993.

Parrinder, Geoffrey, ed. *World Religions: From Ancient History to the Present.* New York: Facts on File, 1971.

"Prison drug smuggling alleged," <http://www.pdxnorml.org/hn__34html>.

Robinson, Rowan. *The Great Book of Hemp: The Complete Guide to the Environmental, Commercial and Medicinal Uses of the World's Most Extraordinary Plant.* Rochester, Vermont: Park Street Press, 1996.

Schultes, Richard E. *Man and Marijuana.* Reprint in *Natural History,* vol. 82, no. 7 (1973) pp. 58–63, 80, 82.

Schultes, Richard E., and A. Hofmann. *Plants of the Gods: Origins of Hallucinogenic Use.* New York: McGraw-Hill, 1979.

Scott, Peter Dale. *Cocaine Politics: Drugs, Armies and the CIA in Central America.* Berkeley: University of California Press, 1991.

————. *The Iran-Contra Connection: Secret Schemes and Covert Operations in the Reagan Era.* Montreal: Black Rose Books, 1987.

The Independent, <www.independent.co.uk/sindypot/stories/cann06.htm>.

U.S. Department of Justice, Drug Enforcement Agency, "In the Matter of Marijuana Rescheduling Petition," [Docket #86-22] (1988, September 6).

Warner, Roger. *The Invisible Hand.* New York: Beech Tree Books, New York, 1968.

Index

About the Author

Joseph Romain holds post-graduate degrees in Philosophy and Library Science. He is the author of eighteen books and editor of or contributor to many more. Mr. Romain has worked as a reference specialist in the areas of philosophy, religion and science. He was the librarian and curator of the National Hockey League's Hall of Fame and Museum for many years. He has been a tavern and folk festival singer, a glazier, a database management consultant and a ghostbuster. Mr. Romain's interests vary rather broadly, and he indulges them without restraint.

He has written widely about the history of sports and popular culture, in particular ice hockey and baseball. His books have sold hundreds of thousands of copies. Romain's novels for younger readers have received praise from readers and acclaim from the industry, winning a Choice Award for his first work of fiction, and first runner up as Canada's Children's Book of the Year for his second.

His interest in the current subject stems from his preoccupation with the history of religion and linguistic anthropology, and from his distaste for stupidity and injustice.

Check out these highlights from our catalog . . .

GRASS: The Paged Experience

Based on the film by Ron Mann; Introduction by Woody Harrelson

GRASS traces the history of North America's prohibition of marijuana, from early 20th-century efforts to demonize the "loco weed" through to the present-day multi-billion-dollar "war on drugs." (ISBN 1-894020-96-0 in Canada; 1-57027-107-0 in the US)

West Coast Smoke

The Inside Story of the B.C. Pot Boom
by Drew Edwards

The first detailed, on-the-ground investigative account of the billion-dollar marijuana industry in the Pacific North West and British Columbia. (1-894040-84-7)

Money for Nothing

Ten Great Ways to Make Money Illegally
by Jeremy Mercer

Crime reporter Jeremy Mercer recounts some of the memorable characters he has met and their ingenious schemes for making money on the wrong side of the law. (1-904020-63-4)

The Vegetarian Traveler

A Guide to Eating Green in 197 Countries
By Bryan Geon

An informed and witty overview of what to expect when attempting to order vegetarian meals all over the globe, along with helpful words and phrases. F or ovo-lacto vegetarians, vegans, and those who simply wish to avoid potentially dangerous foods. (1-894020-85-5)

Warwick Publishing Inc.

Please visit us on the web @ www.warwickgp.com